COOK'S KITCHEN
PIES

igloobooks

Published in 2015
by Igloo Books Ltd
Cottage Farm
Sywell
NN6 0BJ
www.igloobooks.com

Food photography and recipe development: PhotoCuisine UK
Front and back cover images © PhotoCuisine UK

HUN001 1015
2 4 6 8 10 9 7 5 3
ISBN: 978-1-78440-599-1

Printed and manufactured in China

Contents

Pastry

Shortcrust Pastry

MAKES 350 G / 12 OZ

PREPARATION TIME 5 MINUTES

COOKING TIME 40 MINUTES

INGREDIENTS

250 g / 9 oz / 1 ⅔ cups plain (all-purpose) flour, plus extra for dusting

a pinch of salt

125 g / 4 ½ oz / ½ cup unsalted butter, cold and cubed

55 ml / 2 fl. oz / ¼ cup ice cold water

METHOD

- Sift the flour and salt into a food processor. Add the butter and pulse until it resembles fine breadcrumbs.

- Add half of the water and pulse again until a dough starts to come together. Add a little more water if the dough is too dry, pulsing briefly between additions.

- Turn out the dough onto a lightly floured surface and knead gently for 30 seconds until even.

- Flatten the dough and wrap in cling film, then chill for at least 30 minutes.

- Turn out the dough and roll out on a lightly floured surface before using.

Flaky Pastry

MAKES 650 G / 1 LB 7 OZ

PREPARATION TIME 5 MINUTES

COOKING TIME 1 HOUR 10–15 MINUTES

INGREDIENTS

250 g / 9 oz / 1 ⅔ cups strong plain
(all-purpose) flour, plus extra for dusting

¾ tsp salt

250 g / 9 oz / 1 cup unsalted butter, at room
temperature

125–175 ml / 4 ½–6 fl. oz / ½–¾ cup iced
water

METHOD

- Sift the flour and salt into a mixing
  bowl. Break chunks of butter into
  the flour and incorporate with your
  fingertips until it resembles rough
  breadcrumbs.

- Add two-thirds of the water and start
  to mix until a dough forms.

- Cover the dough with cling film and
  chill for 30 minutes. Once rested,
  knead and roll into a 20 cm x 50 cm
  (8 in x 20 in) rectangle on a lightly
  floured surface.

- Fold the top down to the middle
  and bring the bottom end back over
  the fold on top. Turn the dough
  90 degrees and roll out into a 20 cm
  x 50 cm (8 in x 20 in) rectangle as
  above, then repeat the folding step.

- Wrap the pastry in greaseproof paper
  and chill for 30 minutes.

9

Hot Water Pastry

MAKES 450 G / 1 LB

PREPARATION TIME 5 MINUTES

COOKING TIME 1 HOUR 40 MINUTES

INGREDIENTS

250 g / 9 oz / 1 ⅔ cups plain (all-purpose)
  flour, plus extra for dusting

110 ml / 4 fl. oz / ½ cup water

55 g / 2 oz / ¼ cup unsalted butter

3 tbsp lard

½ tsp salt

METHOD

- Sift the flour into a bowl and set to one side. Combine the water, butter, lard and salt in a saucepan, cooking over a medium heat until the fats have melted.

- Pour into the flour and mix with a wooden spoon until a rough dough forms, then cover with a tea towel and leave to rest at room temperature for 1 hour.

- After resting, turn out the dough onto a floured surface and gently knead and fold the dough for 2–3 minutes until even and soft.

- Cover and chill for 30 minutes before turning out and using.

Puff Pastry

MAKES 450 G / 1 LB

PREPARATION TIME 5–10 MINUTES

COOKING TIME 45–50 MINUTES

INGREDIENTS

225 g / 8 oz / 1 ½ cups strong white plain
    flour, plus extra for dusting

a pinch of salt

225 g / 8 oz / 1 cup unsalted butter, cold and
    cubed

110 ml / 4 fl. oz / ½ cup iced water

1 tsp lemon juice

METHOD

- Sift the flour and salt into a large
  mixing bowl.

- Add a quarter of the butter and
  rub into the flour until soft, then
  gradually add the water and the
  lemon juice, mixing until a soft,
  elastic dough forms.

- Roll out the dough on a floured
  surface into a rectangle three times
  as long as it is wide; it should be
  approximately 1 cm (½ in) thick.

- Arrange a quarter of the diced butter
  across the top two-thirds of the
  dough. Fold the bottom third up and
  the top third down, turn 90 degrees
  to the right and seal the edges.

- Repeat this step until all the butter
  has been used up, turning the
  pastry 90 degrees each time.

- Cover and chill before using.

Suet Pastry

MAKES 450 G / 1 LB

PREPARATION TIME 5 MINUTES

COOKING TIME 5–10 MINUTES

INGREDIENTS

300 g / 10 ½ oz / 2 cups self-raising flour
a pinch of salt
150 g / 5 oz / ⅔ cup shredded beef suet
55 ml / 2 fl. oz / ½ cup iced water

METHOD

- Sift the flour and salt into a large mixing bowl.

- Add the suet and stir well to mix, then start to add the water, 1 tbsp at a time. Mix with a knife until the mixture starts to come together as a dough.

- If the dough is too dry, add a little more water and continue to mix until it clumps together.

- Mix the dough with your hands, until smooth and elastic, then use.

Choux Pastry

MAKES 450 G / 1 LB

PREPARATION TIME 5 MINUTES

COOKING TIME 10 MINUTES

INGREDIENTS

150 g / 5 oz / ⅔ cup butter, cubed

300 ml / 10 ½ fl. oz / 1 ¼ cups semi-skimmed milk

1 tsp salt or 1 tsp caster (superfine) sugar

150 g / 5 oz / 1 cup plain (all-purpose) flour, sifted

4 large eggs

METHOD

- Combine the butter, milk and salt or sugar in a saucepan. Warm over a medium heat, stirring occasionally, until the butter has melted and the liquid is simmering.

- Remove from the heat and beat in the flour, stirring constantly, until the dough leaves the sides of the pan.

- Return the saucepan to a medium heat and cook, stirring frequently, for 2 minutes before beating in the eggs, one by one. The pastry should be glossy and of dropping consistency.

- Spoon the pastry into a piping bag fitted with a nozzle before using.

Meat Pies

Meat and Potato Pie

SERVES 6
PREPARATION TIME 20 MINUTES
COOKING TIME 1 HOUR 10–20 MINUTES

INGREDIENTS

2 tbsp sunflower oil

1 large onion, chopped

2 rashers of bacon, chopped

2 small carrots, peeled and sliced

2 large floury potatoes, peeled and diced

600 g / 1 lb / 4 cups beef mince

a dash of Worcestershire sauce

500 ml / 18 fl. oz / 2 cups beef stock

450 g / 1 lb prepared flaky pastry

a little plain (all-purpose) flour, for dusting

1 large egg, beaten

METHOD

- Preheat the oven to 180°C (160°C fan) / 350F / gas 4.

- Heat the oil in a large casserole dish set over a medium heat until hot, then add the onion, bacon, carrot and potato and sweat for 8–10 minutes until softened.

- Add the beef mince and stir well, cooking until browned all over, then add the Worcestershire sauce and cover with the stock.

- Bring to a simmer, then cook over a reduced heat for 15 minutes, stirring occasionally.

- Take two-thirds of the pastry and roll out on a floured surface into a round approximately 1 cm (½ in) thick.

- Use the round of pastry to line the base and sides of a 20 cm (8 in) pie dish that has been lined with greaseproof paper. Prick the base with a fork before chilling.

- Roll out the remaining pastry into a 22 cm (9 in) round approximately 1 cm (½ in) thick. Fill the pastry case with the beef filling, then lift the pastry lid on top and seal against the edge.

- Crimp the rim with the tines of a fork, then brush the top with beaten egg and cut out a small hole in the centre. Bake for 40–50 minutes until the pastry is cooked and golden.

Meat and Vegetable Pie

SERVES 4

PREPARATION TIME 15 MINUTES

COOKING TIME 1 HOUR 35–45 MINUTES

INGREDIENTS

750 g / 1 lb 10 oz / 5 cups chuck steak,
    trimmed and cubed

2 tbsp plain (all-purpose) flour, plus extra
    for dusting

salt and freshly ground black pepper

3 tbsp sunflower oil

1 onion, finely chopped

1 courgette (zucchini), finely diced

75 g / 3 oz / 1 cup button mushrooms, cleaned

150 g / 5 oz / 1 ½ cups peas

500 ml / 18 fl. oz / 2 cups beef stock

150 g / 5 oz prepared shortcrust pastry

1 small egg white, beaten briefly

METHOD

- Dust the beef with the flour and season with salt and pepper. Heat the oil in a large casserole dish set over a moderate heat until hot.

- Seal the beef, in batches, until golden brown, then remove from the dish. Reduce the heat under the dish and add the onion and courgette, sweating them for 4–5 minutes.

- Add the mushrooms and peas and continue to cook for 2 minutes before adding the beef again.

- Cover with the stock, stir well and bring to a simmer. Cook gently for 50–55 minutes until the beef is tender.

- Season to taste, then spoon into a round baking dish. Preheat the oven to 180°C (160°C fan) / 350F / gas 4.

- Roll out the pastry on a lightly floured surface to ½ cm (¼ in) thickness; drape over the dish and seal against the rim, then cut away any excess.

- Cut a small hole in the middle of the pastry. Brush the top with beaten egg white and bake for 25–30 minutes until golden.

- Remove from the oven and leave to stand briefly before serving.

Beef and Ale Pie

SERVES 6

PREPARATION TIME 10–15 MINUTES

COOKING TIME 1 HOUR 35–45 MINUTES

INGREDIENTS

3 tbsp sunflower oil

salt and freshly ground black pepper

750 g / 1 lb 10 oz / 5 cups chuck steak,
    trimmed and cubed

1 onion, finely chopped

500 ml / 18 fl. oz / 2 cups good-quality ale
    or bitter

500 ml / 18 fl. oz / 2 cups beef stock

350 g / 12 oz ready-made shortcrust pastry

a large handful of frozen peas

a little plain (all-purpose) flour, for dusting

1 large egg, beaten

METHOD

- Preheat the oven to 180°C (160°C fan) / 350F / gas 4.

- Heat the oil in a large casserole dish set over a moderate heat until hot. Season the beef steak and seal, in batches, until golden brown all over.

- Remove the beef from the dish and reduce the heat, then pour off all the fat except for 1 tbsp worth. Add the onion and sauté for 3–4 minutes, then return the beef to the dish.

- Add the ale and let it bubble up, then add the stock. Bring to a simmer and cook for 40–45 minutes until the beef is tender.

- Roll out the pastry on a lightly floured surface to 1 cm (½ in) thickness. Use it to cover the base and sides of a 20 cm (8 in) pie dish, letting the excess overhang the sides by 5–6 cm (3 in).

- Prick the base with a fork, then use a slotted spoon to fill with the beef and ale filling. Sprinkle over the peas.

- Fold the overhanging pastry back over the rim, folding and pleating around the edge of the dish.

- Brush the top of the pastry with beaten egg, then bake for 40–45 minutes until golden and cooked.

Beef and Onion Pie

SERVES 4

PREPARATION TIME 15 MINUTES

COOKING TIME 1 HOUR 40–50 MINUTES

INGREDIENTS

2 tbsp sunflower oil

salt and freshly ground black pepper

600 g / 1 lb 5 oz / 4 cups braising steak, diced

2 onions, roughly chopped

125 ml / 4 ½ fl. oz / ½ cup red wine

500 ml / 18 fl. oz / 2 cups beef stock

a small bunch of flat-leaf parsley, chopped

150 g / 5 oz prepared hot water pastry

a little plain (all-purpose) flour, for dusting

1 small egg, beaten

METHOD

- Heat the oil in a ovenproof saucepan set over a moderate heat until hot. Season the steak and seal in the pan until golden brown all over.

- Remove from the pan and reduce the heat a little. Add the onion and sauté for 4–5 minutes, then deglaze the pan with the red wine.

- Return the steak to the pan and cover with the stock. Bring to a simmer and cook for 40–45 minutes until tender, then stir in the parsley.

- Preheat the oven to 180°C (160°C fan) / 350F / gas 4. Roll out the pastry on a lightly floured surface to 1 cm (½ in) thickness and drape over the top of the pan, cutting away some of the excess.

- Reroll the excess pastry and cut into thin strips. Lay over top of the pastry, covering the middle in an interwoven, crosshatch pattern.

- Brush with beaten egg, then place in the oven and bake for 30–35 minutes.

- Remove from the oven and leave to stand for 5 minutes before serving.

TOP TIP

Scrape the base of the pan well after adding the wine to help dislodge any residue.

Beef Wellington

SERVES 4
PREPARATION TIME 20 MINUTES
COOKING TIME 45–55 MINUTES

INGREDIENTS

2 tbsp sunflower oil

650 g / 1 lb 7 oz piece of beef fillet, trimmed

salt and freshly ground black pepper

2 tbsp olive oil

1 clove of garlic, minced

1 shallot, finely chopped

150 g / 5 oz / 2 cups chestnut mushrooms, finely chopped

½ lemon, juiced

a small bunch of flat-leaf parsley, finely chopped

300 g / 10 ½ oz prepared shortcrust pastry

a little plain (all-purpose) flour, for dusting

1 large egg, beaten

METHOD

- Preheat the oven to 180°C (160°C fan) / 350F / gas 4.

- Heat the sunflower oil in a large frying pan set over a moderate heat until hot. Season the beef and seal until golden all over, then remove from the pan.

- Heat the olive oil in a large frying pan set over a medium heat until hot. Sweat the garlic and shallot for 3–4 minutes until softened, then add the mushrooms.

- Continue to cook, stirring occasionally, for 5 minutes, then season to taste with lemon juice, add the parsley and season again.

- Roll out the pastry on a lightly floured surface into a rectangle approximately 25 cm x 15 cm (10 in x 7 in) and 1 cm (½ in) thick. Spread half of the mushrooms over the base and sit the beef fillet on top.

- Spoon the rest of the mushrooms over the beef fillet, then bring the pastry over and around the beef to seal. Decorate the top of the pastry with any leftover pastry strips.

- Transfer to a baking tray and brush with the beaten egg. Bake for 18–22 minutes for medium-rare and another 5–7 minutes for medium.

- Remove from the oven and leave to rest for at least 5 minutes before slicing and serving.

Courgette and Beef Cottage Pie

SERVES 4–6

PREPARATION TIME 15 MINUTES

COOKING TIME 1 HOUR 20–30 MINUTES

INGREDIENTS

2 tbsp olive oil

1 onion, finely chopped

1 stick of celery, finely chopped

2 medium courgettes (zucchinis), sliced

600 g / 1 lb 5 oz / 4 cups beef mince

1 tsp Worcestershire sauce

375 ml / 13 fl. oz / 1 ½ cups beef stock

1 kg / 2 lb 4 oz / 6 ⅔ cups floury potatoes, peeled and diced evenly

75 g / 3 oz / ⅓ cup unsalted butter, softened

salt and freshly ground black pepper

75 g / 3 oz / ¾ cup Parmesan, grated

METHOD

- Heat the olive oil in a large casserole dish set over a medium heat until hot. Sweat the onion and celery for 4–5 minutes, stirring occasionally, until softened.

- Add the sliced courgettes and continue to cook for 3–4 minutes.

- Add the beef mince and brown all over, then add the Worcestershire sauce and beef stock. Bring to a simmer, then cook over a reduced heat for 15–20 minutes.

- Meanwhile, cook the potatoes in a large saucepan of boiling, salted water for 15–20 minutes until tender to the point of a knife.

- Drain and leave to steam dry for a few minutes, then mash with the butter until smooth and season to taste.

- Preheat the oven to 180°C (160°C fan) / 350F / gas 4 and spoon the beef and courgette mixture into the base of a baking dish.

- Spread the mashed potato on top and sprinkle over the Parmesan, then bake for 40–45 minutes until golden on top.

- Remove from the oven and leave to stand for a few minutes before serving.

Steak and Mushroom Pie

SERVES 6

PREPARATION TIME 15 MINUTES

COOKING TIME 1 HOUR 15–20 MINUTES

INGREDIENTS

55 ml / 2 fl. oz / ¼ cup sunflower oil

salt and freshly ground black pepper

1 kg / 2 lb 4 oz / 6 ⅔ cups stewing steak, trimmed and diced

1 tbsp plain (all-purpose) flour, plus extra for dusting

1 onion, finely chopped

150 g / 5 oz / 2 cups closed cap mushrooms, sliced

175 ml / 6 fl. oz / ¾ cup beer

750 ml / 1 pint 6 fl. oz / 3 cups beef stock

a small bunch of flat-leaf parsley, roughly chopped

250 g / 9 oz prepared puff pastry

1 large egg, beaten

METHOD

- Heat the oil in a large casserole dish set over a moderate heat until hot. Season the steak and seal, in batches, until golden brown all over.

- Remove the steak from the dish and pour off any excess oil so that you have 2 tbsp left; sprinkle the flour over the sealed steak.

- Add the onions and mushrooms. Sauté for 3–4 minutes, stirring occasionally, then deglaze with the beer and return the steak to the dish.

- Cover with the stock and bring to a simmer. Cook at a steady simmer for 45–50 minutes until tender, then stir through the parsley and season to taste.

- Preheat the oven to 190°C (170°C fan) / 375F / gas 5 and spoon the beef and mushrooms into a rectangular baking dish.

- Roll out the pastry on a lightly floured surface into a rectangle slightly larger than the baking dish; drape over the top of the beef filling and seal against the rim.

- Score a light pattern on the top of the pastry using a knife. Brush with beaten egg and bake for 20–25 minutes until golden on top.

- Remove from the oven and leave to stand for 5 minutes before serving.

Steak and Kidney Pie

SERVES 6

PREPARATION TIME 15–20 MINUTES

COOKING TIME 2–2 ¼ HOURS

INGREDIENTS

3 tbsp sunflower oil

750 g / 1 lb 10 oz / 5 cups stewing steak, trimmed and evenly diced

1 onion, chopped

250 g / 9 oz / 1 ⅔ cups lamb's kidneys, cored and diced

2 tbsp plain (all-purpose) flour, plus extra for dusting

850 ml / 1 pint 10 fl. oz / 3 ½ cups beef stock

a dash of Worcestershire sauce

salt and freshly ground black pepper

a small bunch of flat-leaf parsley, finely chopped

200 g / 7 oz prepared flaky pastry

1 small egg, beaten

METHOD

- Heat the oil in a large casserole dish set over a moderate heat until hot.

- Season the steak and seal in batches, until golden all over, then remove from the dish and drain on kitchen paper.

- Reduce the heat under the dish and sauté the onion in the accumulated oil for 3–4 minutes until golden.

- Return the steak to the dish along with the kidneys and flour. Stir well and cook for 1 minute, then cover with the stock and Worcestershire sauce.

- Bring to a simmer and cook steadily for 1 ¼–½ hours, uncovered, until the steak is tender.

- Adjust the seasoning to taste and stir through the parsley, then spoon into a square baking dish. Preheat the oven to 220°C (200°C fan) / 425F / gas 7.

- Roll out the pastry on a lightly floured surface into a rectangle slightly larger than the dish, then drape over the beef filling. Seal against the edges and cut away any excess.

- Brush the top with the beaten egg and bore a small hole in the centre. Bake for 25–30 minutes until golden and risen.

Pork and Cider Pie

SERVES 4
PREPARATION TIME 15–20 MINUTES
COOKING TIME 1 HOUR 45–50 MINUTES

INGREDIENTS

3 tbsp sunflower oil

salt and freshly ground black pepper

650 g / 1 lb 7 oz / 4 ⅓ cups pork shoulder,
    trimmed and diced

2 large onions, finely sliced

2 large Bramley apples, cored, peeled and
    sliced

250 ml / 9 fl. oz / 1 cup cider

550 ml / 1 pint / 2 ¼ cups ham stock

200 g / 7 oz prepared hot water pastry

a little plain (all-purpose) flour, for dusting

1 small egg, beaten

METHOD

- Preheat the oven to 180°C (160°C fan) / 350F / gas 4.

- Heat the oil in a large saucepan set over a moderate heat until hot. Season the pork, then seal in batches until golden brown.

- Remove from the saucepan and reduce the heat a little, then add the onion and apple. Sweat for 5 minutes, then deglaze with the cider.

- Add the pork back to the saucepan and cover with the stock. Bring to a simmer and braise gently for 40–45 minutes until tender, then season and strain into a large, round baking dish.

- Roll out the pastry on a lightly floured surface to 1 cm (½ in) thickness; cut it to shape and lay over the pork filling, then brush the top with beaten egg.

- Bake for 35–45 minutes until golden and cooked through, then remove from the oven and leave to stand for 5 minutes before serving.

TOP TIP
Strain the pork filling well before spooning into the dish to prevent a soggy pastry crust.

Pork Pie

SERVES 8

PREPARATION TIME 10 MINUTES

COOKING TIME 2 HOURS 15–20 MINUTES

INGREDIENTS

450 g / 1 lb / 3 cups diced pork shoulder

600 g / 1 lb 5 oz / 4 cups pork mince

2 tsp Worcestershire sauce

1 tsp ground allspice

1 tsp dried sage

salt and freshly ground black pepper

450 g / 1 lb prepared hot water pastry

a little plain (all-purpose) flour, for dusting

1 egg, lightly beaten

METHOD

- Preheat the oven to 160°C (140°C fan) / 325F / gas 3.

- Pulse the pork shoulder in a food processor until finely chopped, then add the pork mince, Worcestershire sauce, allspice and sage and pulse again until thoroughly combined.

- Season generously and set to one side.

- Take two-thirds of the pastry and roll out on a lightly floured surface to a 30 cm (12 in) round, about 1 cm (½ in) thickness.

- Use the pastry to line the base and sides of a 20 cm (8 in) pie dish. Fill with the pork mixture and roll the remaining pastry into a 20 cm (8 in) round, approximately 1 cm (½ in) thick.

- Drape over the pork filling and seal against the side of the pastry, then brush with beaten egg.

- Bake for 1 ½ hours, then remove and brushing the top with beaten egg; return to the oven for 30 minutes.

- Remove to a wire rack to cool before turning out and serving.

TOP TIP

Take a reading from the centre of the pie; it must reach 63°C / 145F before serving.

Sausage and Apple Pie

MAKES 4

PREPARATION TIME 20 MINUTES

COOKING TIME 20–25 MINUTES

INGREDIENTS

450 g / 1 lb / 3 cups pork sausages, skinned

1 onion, finely chopped

2 large Bramley apples, peeled, cored and
    finely diced

a few sprigs of sage, finely chopped

salt and freshly ground black pepper

250 g / 9 oz prepared flaky pastry

a little plain (all-purpose) flour, for dusting

1 small egg, beaten

METHOD

- Preheat the oven to 180°C (160°C fan) / 350F / gas 4.

- Remove the sausage meat from the skins and mix with the onion, apple, sage and seasoning in a large mixing bowl.

- Divide the mixture between 4 individual heatproof ramekins.

- Roll out the pastry on a lightly floured surface to 1 cm (½ in) thickness and cut out 4 rounds of pastry to act as lids on top of the filling.

- Wet the rims of the ramekins with a little water, then drape the pastry over them. Press down gently and cut away any excess pastry from the rims.

- Brush the tops with beaten egg and arrange on a baking tray. Bake for 20–25 minutes until golden brown and slightly risen.

- Remove to a wire rack to cool before serving.

TOP TIP
To skin the sausages, run the tip of a sharp knife down the lengths of their skins.

Tagine Pot Pie

SERVES 4

PREPARATION TIME 15 MINUTES

COOKING TIME 1 HOUR 40–50 MINUTES

INGREDIENTS

3 tbsp olive oil

salt and freshly ground black pepper

750 g / 1 lb 10 oz / 5 cups lamb shoulder, diced

1 onion, finely chopped

2 carrots, peeled and diced

1 tbsp harissa paste

500 ml / 18 fl. oz / 2 cups lamb stock

2 tbsp white sesame seeds

200 g / 7 oz prepared shortcrust pastry

a little plain (all-purpose) flour, for dusting

1 large egg yolk

a small handful of mint leaves, to garnish

METHOD

- Heat the olive oil in a large casserole dish set over a medium heat until hot. Season the lamb and seal in batches until golden brown, then remove from the dish.

- Reduce the heat slightly, then add the onion, carrot and a little salt. Sweat for 5–6 minutes until softened.

- Stir through the harissa and return the lamb to the dish. Cover with the stock and bring to a simmer.

- Cook gently for 50–60 minutes until the lamb is tender. Season to taste, then spoon into a round baking dish and top with half the sesame seeds.

- Preheat the oven to 180°C (160°C fan) / 350F / gas 4. Roll out the pastry on a lightly floured surface to 1 cm (½ in) thickness, then drape over the baking dish.

- Seal well against the rim, cutting away any excess.

- Beat the egg yolk with 1 tbsp of water and brush over the pastry and rim. Make a few incisions in the pastry with a sharp knife and top with the remaining sesame seeds.

- Bake for 25–30 minutes until the pastry is golden and cooked; garnish with mint leaves before serving.

Bacon and Egg Pie

SERVES 4

PREPARATION TIME 25 MINUTES

COOKING TIME 40 MINUTES

INGREDIENTS

450 g / 1 lb / 3 cups floury potatoes,
    peeled and sliced

2 large eggs

4 rashers of back bacon, chopped

150 ml / 5 fl. oz / ⅔ cup double (heavy) cream

salt and freshly ground black pepper

200 g / 7 oz prepared shortcrust pastry

a little plain (all-purpose) flour, for dusting

METHOD

- Cook the potato slices in a large saucepan of salted, boiling water for 12–15 minutes until tender to the point of a knife.

- Meanwhile, cook the eggs in a separate saucepan of boiling water for 12 minutes, then drain and refresh in iced water.

- Drain the potato when ready and leave to steam dry for a few minutes. Peel and chop the eggs and combine with the potato slices, bacon, cream and seasoning in a mixing bowl.

- Divide the mixture between 4 individual ramekins and arrange on a baking tray.

- Preheat the oven to 160°C (140°C fan) / 325F / gas 3.

- Roll out the pastry on a lightly floured surface to 1 cm (½ in) thickness. Cut out 4 rounds and drape over the filling in the ramekins.

- Seal the pastry against the ramekins by pushing against the edges with your thumb. Bore a small hole in the centres.

- Bake for 20–25 minutes until the pastry is golden and cooked through. Remove to a wire rack to cool before serving.

Shepherd's Pie

SERVES 6

PREPARATION TIME 25 MINUTES

COOKING TIME 50–60 MINUTES

INGREDIENTS

2 tbsp sunflower oil

1 large green pepper, deseeded and finely diced

1 onion, finely chopped

500 g / 1 lb 2 oz / 3 ⅓ cups lamb mince

75 g / 3 oz / 1 ½ cups baby spinach, washed

2 tsp Worcestershire sauce

250 ml / 9 fl. oz / 1 cup lamb stock

1 kg / 2 lb 4 oz / 6 ⅔ cups floury potatoes, peeled and cut into chunks

2 courgettes (zucchinis), cut into large chunks

salt and freshly ground black pepper

100 g / 3 ½ oz / 1 cup Cheddar, grated

a few sprigs of thyme, to garnish

METHOD

- Heat the oil in a large casserole dish set over a medium heat, then add the pepper and onion and sweat for 6–8 minutes.

- Increase the heat and add the lamb mince. Leave to brown for 2–3 minutes, then stir well.

- Add the spinach and Worcestershire sauce. Stir well and cover with the stock, then cook at a simmer for 15 minutes.

- Meanwhile, cook the potatoes in a large saucepan of salted, boiling water for 15–20 minutes until tender. Add the courgette chunks to the water 5 minutes before the potato is ready.

- Drain well and mash with seasoning until smooth. Preheat the oven to 190°C (170°C fan) / 375F / gas 5 and spoon the lamb into an oval baking dish.

- Top with the mashed potato and courgette, then smooth the top and sprinkle over the cheese.

- Bake for 25–30 minutes until golden on top. Remove from the oven and leave to stand for 5 minutes, then garnish with thyme and serve.

Lamb and Mint Pie

SERVES 4

PREPARATION TIME 15 MINUTES

COOKING TIME 50–60 MINUTES

INGREDIENTS

3 tbsp sunflower oil

salt and freshly ground black pepper

600 g / 1 lb 5 oz / 4 cups lamb neck fillet,
    trimmed and diced

1 large carrot, peeled and sliced

1 onion, chopped

1 fennel bulb, trimmed and sliced

1 red pepper, deseeded and diced

2 tsp dried mint

250 ml / 9 fl. oz / 1 cup lamb stock

150 g / 5 oz prepared shortcrust pastry

a little plain (all-purpose) flour, for dusting

METHOD

- Preheat the oven to 190°C (170°C fan) / 375F / gas 5. Heat the oil in a casserole dish set over a moderate heat until hot.

- Season the lamb and seal in batches until golden brown, then remove from the dish and reduce the heat a little.

- Add the carrot, onion and fennel and sweat for 4–5 minutes, stirring occasionally.

- Add the pepper and 1 tsp of dried mint, stirring well, then return the lamb and cover with the stock.

- Bring to a simmer and cook gently for 15 minutes, then season and spoon into a 20 cm (8 in) round baking dish.

- Roll out the pastry on a lightly floured surface into a 22 cm (9 in) round, approximately ½ cm (¼ in) thick. Drape over the baking dish and seal against the rim, cutting away any excess.

- Make incisions across the pastry before baking for 20–25 minutes until golden. Remove to a wire rack to cool before garnishing with the rest of the dried mint.

MEAT PIES

Lamb, Pea and Potato Pie

SERVES 6
PREPARATION TIME 20 MINUTES
COOKING TIME 1 HOUR 5–10 MINUTES

INGREDIENTS

2 tbsp sunflower oil

1 onion, finely chopped

2 cloves of garlic, minced

salt and freshly ground black pepper

600 g / 1 lb 5 oz / 4 cups lamb mince

125 ml / 4 ½ fl. oz / ½ cup red wine

500 ml / 18 fl. oz / 2 cups lamb stock

450 g / 1 lb / 3 cups new potatoes, sliced

150 g / 5 oz / 1 ½ cups frozen peas

225 g / 8 oz prepared puff pastry

a little plain (all-purpose) flour, for dusting

1 large egg, beaten

METHOD

- Heat the oil in a large casserole dish set over a medium heat until hot. Add the onion, garlic and a little salt, sweating for 5–6 minutes until softened.

- Increase the heat a little and add the lamb mince. Brown well, breaking it up with a wooden spoon.

- Once browned, deglaze with the red wine and cover with the stock, then bring to a simmer.

- Stir in the potatoes and cook steadily for 20–25 minutes, then add the peas and season to taste.

- Spoon into a large, rectangular baking dish and preheat the oven to 190°C (170°C fan) / 375F / gas 5.

- Roll out the pastry on a lightly floured surface to ½ cm (¼ in) thickness. Drape over the baking dish and seal against the edges.

- Trim any excess pastry and brush the top with the beaten egg, then score a light pattern in the pastry using a sharp knife.

- Bake for 25–30 minutes until golden and puffed before serving.

TOP TIP

When deglazing the dish, scrape the base well to dislodge as any residue.

Lamb and Apricot Pie

SERVES 6

PREPARATION TIME 25 MINUTES

COOKING TIME 2 HOURS 5–10 MINUTES

INGREDIENTS

400 g / 14 oz prepared shortcrust pastry

a little plain (all-purpose) flour, for dusting

3 tbsp sunflower oil

750 g / 1 lb 10 oz / 5 cups lamb neck fillet,
    trimmed and cubed

1 onion, finely chopped

salt and freshly ground black pepper

2 tsp ras el hanout

1 tsp paprika

225 g / 8 oz / 1 ½ cups dried apricots, chopped

500 ml / 18 fl. oz / 2 cups lamb stock

1 small egg, beaten

METHOD

- Roll out two-thirds of the pastry on a lightly floured surface to 1 cm (½ in) thickness and use to line the base and sides of a 20 cm (8 in) springform cake tin.

- Trim any excess pastry and prick the base with a fork, then chill.

- Heat the oil in a large casserole dish set over a moderate heat until hot. Season the lamb and seal in batches until golden all over.

- Remove the lamb from the dish and reduce the heat slightly, then add the onion and a little salt and sweat for 4–5 minutes.

- Stir in the spices and apricots, then return the lamb to the dish. Cover with the stock and bring to a simmer.

- Cook gently for 1 hour 5–10 minutes until the lamb is very tender. Use a couple of forks to shred the lamb and season to taste.

- Strain the liquid from the lamb and apricot, then spoon the filling into the chilled pastry. Preheat the oven to 180°C (160°C fan) / 350F / gas 4.

- Roll out the remaining pastry to 1 cm (½ in) thickness. Drape over the cake tin and seal against the side of the lined pastry.

- Brush the top with beaten egg, then bake for 40–45 minutes until golden and cooked before serving.

Game Pie

METHOD

- Preheat the oven to 180°C (160°C fan) / 350F / gas 4. Heat the oil in a large casserole dish set over a moderate heat until hot.

- Season the meats and seal in batches until golden brown, then remove from the dish. Deglaze the dish with the Cognac, then tip the liquid and meat into a food processor.

- Add the parsley and seasoning and pulse until the mixture comes together.

- Roll out a piece of the pastry on a lightly floured surface into a 30 cm (12 in) round approximately ½ cm (¼ in) thick.

- Lift onto a baking tray and top with the game mixture, leaving a 2 cm (1 in) border all the way around.

- Roll out the other piece of pastry to the same dimensions as the first piece. Brush the border of the pastry base with beaten egg, then drape the other round of pastry over the filling.

- Seal the edges and brush the top with the rest of the beaten egg, then bake for 40–45 minutes until golden brown.

- Remove from the oven and leave to cool before serving.

SERVES 6
PREPARATION TIME 25 MINUTES
COOKING TIME 55–60 MINUTES

INGREDIENTS

- tbsp sunflower oil
- salt and freshly ground black pepper
- 450 g / 1 lb / 3 cups venison loin, trimmed and diced
- 350 g / 12 oz / 2 ⅓ cups skinless pigeon or grouse breast, trimmed and diced
- tbsp Cognac or brandy
- small bunch of flat-leaf parsley, chopped
- 350 g / 12 oz prepared flaky pastry, divided in two
- large egg, beaten

Pheasant Pie

MAKES 4
PREPARATION TIME 20 MINUTES
COOKING TIME 45–50 MINUTES

INGREDIENTS

2 tbsp unsalted butter

2 tbsp plain (all-purpose) flour, plus extra
  for dusting

600 ml / 1 pint 2 fl. oz / 2 ½ cups whole
  (full-fat) milk

1 bay leaf

450 g / 1 lb / 3 cups skinless pheasant breast,
  diced

150 g / 5 oz / 2 cups morel mushrooms,
  cleaned

225 g / 8 oz prepared puff pastry

a little plain (all-purpose) flour, for dusting

1 large egg, beaten

salt and freshly ground black pepper

METHOD

- Melt the butter in a large saucepan set over a medium heat until hot. Whisk in the flour and cook until you have a golden roux.

- Add the milk in a slow, steady stream, whisking constantly, until you have a smooth sauce, then add the bay leaf and pheasant.

- Simmer for 10 minutes, stirring occasionally, then add the morels and season to taste. Spoon into 4 individual ramekins and arrange on a baking tray.

- Preheat the oven to 190°C (170°C fan) / 375F / gas 5.

- Roll out the pastry on a lightly floured surface to ½ cm (¼ in) thickness and cut out 4 rounds that will fit as lids on top of the ramekins.

- Drape the rounds over the filling and seal against the rims, using a little beaten egg on the rim to help seal them.

- Brush the tops of the pastry with more beaten egg and bake for 20–25 minutes until golden and puffed.

- Remove from the oven and leave to stand for 5 minutes before serving.

Rabbit Pie

SERVES 6–8

PREPARATION TIME 25 MINUTES

COOKING TIME 2 HOURS 20–30 MINUTES

INGREDIENTS

3 tbsp sunflower oil

salt and freshly ground black pepper

750 g / 1 lb 10 oz / 5 cups rabbit loin, diced

2 cloves of garlic, minced

2 tbsp Cognac or brandy

a dash of Worcestershire sauce

500 g / 1 lb 2 oz prepared hot water pastry

a little plain (all-purpose) flour, for dusting

250 g / 9 oz / 1 ⅔ cup foie gras, de-veined and
    cut into chunks

1 tbsp green peppercorns in brine, drained

2 large egg yolks, beaten

METHOD

- Heat the oil in a large casserole dish set over a moderate heat until hot. Season the rabbit and seal in batches until golden all over, then transfer to a food processor.

- Add the garlic, Cognac and Worcestershire sauce and blitz until combined.

- Take two-thirds of the pastry and roll out on a lightly floured surface into a 30 cm (12 in) round, approximately 1 cm (½ in) thick.

- Use it to line a rimmed 20 cm (8 in) pie dish. Spoon half of the rabbit mixture into the base, then top with the foie gras and peppercorns.

- Pack the rest of the rabbit mixture on top and smooth with the back of a tablespoon. Roll out the remaining pastry into a 22 cm (9 in) round, approximately 1 cm (½ in) thick.

- Drape over the filling and crimp against the other piece of pastry using a little water to help. Preheat the oven to 160°C (140°C fan) / 325F / gas 3.

- Bake the pie for 1 ½ hours, then remove from the oven and carefully loosen the pie from the dish and invert onto a baking tray.

- Score a pattern on the pastry, then brush with the remaining egg yolk and return to the oven for 30 minutes to brown.

- Leave to cool for 5 minutes before serving.

Poultry Pies

Chicken and Mushroom Pie

MAKES 4

PREPARATION TIME 15 MINUTES

COOKING TIME 40–50 MINUTES

INGREDIENTS

2 tbsp sunflower oil

1 large leek, sliced

salt and freshly ground black pepper

2 large skinless chicken breasts, diced

250 g / 9 oz / 3 cups closed cup mushrooms,
   roughly chopped

500 ml / 18 fl. oz / 2 cups chicken stock

110 g/ 4 oz / 1 cup frozen peas

2 sheets of filo pastry

2 tbsp unsalted butter, melted

METHOD

- Preheat the oven to 190°C (170°C fan) / 375F / gas 5 and heat the oil in a saucepan set over a medium heat.

- Add the leek and some seasoning and sweat for 4–5 minutes, stirring occasionally.

- Add the chicken and mushrooms and cook for a further 4–5 minutes, then cover with the stock.

- Bring to a simmer and cook steadily for 8–10 minutes, then stir through the peas and season to taste.

- Spoon into individual ramekins. Use a sharp knife to cut out rounds of filo pastry.

- Wet the rims of the ramekins with melted butter and top with the rounds of pastry, then brush the tops with more melted butter.

- Bake for 15–20 minutes until the pastry is golden and cooked, then remove from the oven and leave to stand briefly before serving.

TOP TIP
Keep the filo pastry under a damp tea towel to prevent it from drying out.

Curried Chicken Pie

METHOD

- Preheat the oven to 180°C (160°C fan) / 350F / gas 4. Melt the butter in a large saucepan set over a medium heat.

- Add the leek, garlic and a little salt and sweat for 6–7 minutes, stirring occasionally, until softened.

- Add the curry powder. Stir well, and cook for 1 minute, then add the chicken.

- Cover with the stock and bring to a simmer. Cook for 5 minutes, then stir through the cream, parsley and some seasoning.

- Spoon into a large cast-iron pan or baking dish. Roll out the pastry on a lightly floured surface into a round approximately 1 cm (½ in) thick.

- Drape over the filling and seal against the inside edge of the pan or dish. Cut away any excess and bore a small hole in the middle.

- Brush with beaten egg and bake for 20–25 minutes until puffed and golden, then serve.

SERVES 4

PREPARATION TIME 20 MINUTES

COOKING TIME 40–45 MINUTES

INGREDIENTS

2 tbsp unsalted butter

1 large leek, sliced

2 cloves of garlic, minced

salt and freshly ground black pepper

1 tbsp Madras curry powder

4 small skinless chicken breasts, diced

375 ml / 13 fl. oz / 1 ½ cups chicken stock

375 ml / 13 fl. oz / 1 ½ cups double (heavy) cream

a small handful of flat-leaf parsley, finely chopped

250 g / 9 oz prepared puff pastry

a little plain (all-purpose) flour, for dusting

1 small egg, beaten

TOP TIP

Boring a hole will help steam to escape from the pastry and aid in rising.

Chicken and Lemon Pie

SERVES 4

PREPARATION TIME 25 MINUTES

COOKING TIME 1 HOUR 20–25 MINUTES

INGREDIENTS

350 g / 12 oz prepared shortcrust pastry

a little plain (all-purpose) flour, for dusting

3 tbsp olive oil

1 onion, finely chopped

2 cloves of garlic, minced

salt and freshly ground black pepper

4 large skinless chicken breasts, diced

150 g / 5 oz / 1 cup pitted green olives

150 g / 5 oz / 3 cups chopped kale

1 preserved lemon, drained and chopped

a few sprigs of rosemary, finely chopped

METHOD

- Preheat the oven to 160°C (140°C fan) / 325F / gas 3. Roll out two-thirds of the pastry on a lightly floured surface to ½ cm (¼ in) thickness.

- Use the pastry to line a 20 cm (8 in) pie dish, cutting away the excess and pressing well into the base and sides.

- Prick the base with a fork, then chill until ready to fill.

- Heat the oil in a large casserole dish set over a medium heat until hot. Add the onion, garlic and a little salt, sweating for 5–6 minutes until softened.

- Add the chicken, olives, kale and preserved lemon and continue to cook for a further 7–8 minutes, stirring occasionally, then season.

- Stir through most of the rosemary, then spoon the filling into the lined pastry with a slotted spoon. Roll out the remaining pastry to the same thickness as before.

- Drape over the filling and crimp against the inside of the lined pastry. Cut away the excess and cut out a small hole in the middle.

- Bake for 55–60 minutes until the pastry is golden and cooked. Garnish with the remaining rosemary sprinkled on top, then serve.

Chicken, Ham and Leek Pie

SERVES 4

PREPARATION TIME 15 MINUTES

COOKING TIME 40–45 MINUTES

INGREDIENTS

- tbsp unsalted butter
- 2 small carrots, peeled and diced
- 2 large skinless chicken breasts, diced
- 150 g / 5 oz / 1 cup cooked gammon steak, cubed
- 375 ml / 13 fl. oz / 1 ½ cups ham stock
- 250 ml / 9 fl. oz / 1 cup double (heavy) cream
- 150 g / 5 oz / 1 ½ cups frozen peas
- 150 g / 5 oz prepared puff pastry
- a little plain (all-purpose) flour, for dusting
- 1 large egg, beaten

METHOD

- Melt the butter in a large saucepan set over a medium heat until hot. Add the carrot and sweat for 3–4 minutes.

- Add the chicken and gammon steak, then cook for a further 4–5 minutes, stirring occasionally, before covering with the stock.

- Bring to a simmer and cook for another 5 minutes, then stir in the cream and peas. Simmer for 2 minutes, then pour into a round pie dish.

- Preheat the oven to 180°C (160°C fan) / 350F / gas 4.

- Roll out the pastry on a lightly floured surface into a 1 cm (½ in) thick round. Drape over the filling in the dish and seal against the inside rim, cutting away any excess pastry.

- Brush the top with beaten egg and score a crosshatch pattern using a sharp knife. Bake for 20–25 minutes until golden and risen, then serve.

TOP TIP

Adjust the amount of cream as necessary to get the right consistency.

Duck and Sweet Potato Pie

SERVES 4–6

PREPARATION TIME 15 MINUTES

COOKING TIME 2 HOURS 5–10 MINUTES

INGREDIENTS

4 duck legs on the bone

salt and freshly ground black pepper

2 tbsp sunflower oil

750 g / 1 lb 10 oz / 5 cups sweet potatoes,
    peeled and cut into chunks

110 g / 4 oz / ½ cup unsalted butter, cubed

75 g / 3 oz / 1 cup Parmesan, grated

75 g / 3 oz / 1 cup fresh breadcrumbs

METHOD

- Preheat the oven to 190°C (170°C fan) / 375F / gas 5. Place the duck legs on a baking tray and prick the skin with a wooden skewer.

- Season with salt and pepper, then drizzle with sunflower oil. Roast for 1 hour 20–30 minutes until the skin is golden and crisp.

- Remove from the oven and leave to rest, covered loosely with aluminium foil, for 15 minutes.

- Meanwhile, cook the sweet potatoes in a large saucepan of salted, boiling water for 15–20 minutes until tender to the point of a knife.

- Drain well and leave to cool slightly, then mash with the butter and seasoning until smooth.

- Shred the duck meat from the legs, discarding the skin and bones, and arrange in the base of an oval baking dish.

- Top with the sweet potato mash and sprinkle over the Parmesan and breadcrumbs.

- Bake for 30–35 minutes until golden on top, then serve immediately.

TOP TIP
The sweet potato chunks should be evenly cut into 5 cm (2 in) cubes.

Duck Pie

MAKES 4

PREPARATION TIME 20 MINUTES

COOKING TIME 1 HOUR 40–45 MINUTES

INGREDIENTS

2 tbsp sunflower oil

2 large onions, chopped

1 clove of garlic, finely chopped

1 stick of celery, finely chopped

2 medium carrots, peeled and chopped

2 large duck legs

2 tsp Worcestershire sauce

750 ml / 1 pint 6 fl. oz / 3 cups chicken stock

300 g / 10 ½ oz prepared puff pastry

a little plain (all-purpose) flour, for dusting

1 large egg, beaten

salt and freshly ground black pepper

METHOD

- Heat the oil in a large casserole dish set over a medium heat until hot. Add the onion, garlic, celery, carrot and a little salt and sweat for 7–8 minutes until softened.

- Add the duck legs and Worcestershire sauce and cook for 2 minutes, stirring occasionally, before covering with the stock.

- Bring to a simmer and cook gently, covered, for 1 hour, then remove the duck legs and shred the meat back into the vegetables and gravy.

- Preheat the oven to 190°C (170°C fan) / 375F / gas 5. Roll out half of the pastry on a lightly floured surface to 1 cm (½ in) thickness and use it to line the base and sides of a round baking dish.

- Trim any excess overhanging pastry, then spoon the duck meat and vegetables into the pastry.

- Roll out the remaining pastry and drape over the filing, sealing against the side of the lined pastry.

- Brush with the beaten egg and bake for 25–30 minutes until golden and puffed, then serve.

TOP TIP
Use a slotted spoon to spoon the duck filling into the pastry.

Turkey Pie

MAKES 4

PREPARATION TIME 15–20 MINUTES

COOKING TIME 45–50 MINUTES

INGREDIENTS

1 kg / 2 lb 4 oz / 6 ⅔ cups floury potatoes,
    peeled and diced

4 medium Bramley apples, peeled, cored
    and diced

2 tbsp caster (superfine) sugar

75 g / 3 oz / ⅓ cup butter, softened

55 ml / 2 fl. oz / ¼ cup double (heavy) cream

salt and freshly ground black pepper

2 tbsp sunflower oil

4 large turkey breast escalopes

1 Braeburn apple, cored and finely diced

METHOD

- Cook the potatoes in a large saucepan of salted, boiling water for 15–20 minutes until tender to the point of a knife.

- Meanwhile, place the Bramley apples and sugar in a large saucepan with 2 tbsp of cold water.

- Cover and cook over a medium heat until soft enough to break with a wooden spoon, then remove from the heat and mash briefly into a purée.

- Drain the potatoes and leave to steam for a few minutes, then mash with the butter, cream and seasoning.

- Preheat the oven to 190°C (170°C fan) / 375F / gas 5.

- Heat the sunflower oil in a large frying pan set over a moderate heat until hot. Season the turkey escalopes and seal for 1 minute on both sides before removing from the pan.

- Spoon the apple purée into the base of 4 individual baking dishes. Top with the turkey and then a layer of mashed potato.

- Sprinkle over the diced Braeburn apple and bake for 15 minutes before serving.

Turkey Leftover Pie

SERVES 8

PREPARATION TIME 20 MINUTES

COOKING TIME 1 HOUR 30–40 MINUTES

INGREDIENTS

400 g / 14 oz prepared hot water pastry

a little plain (all-purpose) flour, for dusting

450 g / 1 lb / 3 cups leftover turkey meat, sliced

225 g / 8 oz / 1 ½ cups leftover ham, sliced

225 g / 8 oz / 1 ½ cups leftover stuffing

110 g / 4 oz / ½ cup cranberry sauce

1 small egg, beaten

salt and freshly ground black pepper

METHOD

- Preheat the oven to 160°C (140°C fan) / 325F / gas 3.

- Roll out two-thirds of the pastry on a lightly floured surface to 1 cm (½ in) thickness and use it to line a 20 cm (8 in) springform cake tin.

- Press well into the base and sides and trim the excess. Prick the base with a fork and fill with a combination of the leftover meats, stuffing and cranberry sauce.

- Roll out the remaining pastry and drape over the filling. Seal against the side of the lined pastry, trimming away the excess.

- Brush the top with beaten egg and bore a small hole in the middle, then bake for 1 hour 30–40 minutes until the pastry is golden and cooked.

- Remove to a wire rack to cool before turning out and serving.

TOP TIP
Use a combination of turkey breast and leg meat for the best taste.

Fish and Seafood Pies

Smoked Salmon and Herb Pie

SERVES 6–8
PREPARATION TIME 25 MINUTES
COOKING TIME 1 HOUR 15–20 MINUTES

INGREDIENTS

750 g / 1 lb 10 oz / 5 cups smoked salmon fillet
225 ml / 8 fl. oz / 1 cup dry white wine
150 ml / 5 fl. oz / ⅔ cup water
1 bay leaf
6 small eggs
salt and freshly ground black pepper
350 g / 12 oz / 2 ⅓ cups cooked long-grain rice
a large bunch of chives
350 g / 12 oz prepared shortcrust pastry
a little plain (all-purpose) flour, for dusting

METHOD

- Place the salmon fillet in a large saucepan and add the white wine, water and bay leaf. Bring to a simmer, cover and cook for 8–10 minutes until cooked through, then drain.

- Preheat the oven to 180°C (160°C fan) / 350F / gas 4. Cook the eggs in a large saucepan of boiling water for 10 minutes.

- Drain the eggs and refresh in iced water. Flake the salmon into a large mixing bowl and season with salt and pepper.

- Place the rice in a large mixing bowl. Finely chop half of the chives and stir into the rice with salt and pepper.

- Roll out two-thirds of the pastry on a lightly floured surface into a large rectangle approximately 1 cm (½ in) thick and use it to line a 900 g / 2 lb rectangular loaf or baking tin.

- Fill the base with half of the rice. Top with half of the salmon, then peel the eggs and lay down the middle of the salmon.

- Top with more salmon and the remaining rice. Roll out the remaining pastry and drape over the filing, then crimp against the edge of the lined pastry.

- Bake for 40–45 minutes until the pastry is golden and cooked through, then garnish with the remaining chives and serve.

Salmon and Potato Pie

SERVES 6

PREPARATION TIME 15–20 MINUTES

COOKING TIME 1 HOUR 5–15 MINUTES

INGREDIENTS

400 g / 14 oz / 2 ⅔ cups skinless salmon fillet, diced

250 ml / 9 fl. oz / 1 cup fish stock

1 bay leaf

1 tsp dried dill

750 g / 1 lb 10 oz / 5 cups floury potatoes, peeled and sliced

350 g / 12 oz prepared hot water pastry

a little plain (all-purpose) flour, for dusting

1 large egg, beaten

METHOD

- Place the salmon fillet in a large saucepan and cover with the fish stock and 150 ml / 5 fl. oz / ⅔ cup of water. Add the bay leaf and dill and bring to a simmer over a medium heat.

- Cover and cook for 5–6 minutes until cooked through. Remove from the heat and strain the fish.

- Preheat the oven to 180°C (160°C fan) / 350F / gas 4. Bring a large saucepan of salted water to the boil and cook the potato slices for 6–7 minutes until tender to the point of a knife.

- Drain and leave to dry. Roll out two-thirds of the pastry on a lightly floured surface into a large round approximately 1 cm (½ in) thick.

- Use the round of pastry to line the base and sides of a 20 cm (8 in) pie dish. Flake the cooked salmon and spoon onto the base, then top with the potato slices.

- Roll out the remaining pastry to a round approximately 1 cm (½ in) thick. Drape over the filling and crimp against the edge of the pastry, then brush with the beaten egg.

- Bake for 45–50 minutes until the pastry is golden and cooked, then serve.

Salmon and Prawn Pie

METHOD

- Heat the olive oil in a large saucepan set over a medium heat until hot. Add the leek and a little salt and sweat for 4–5 minutes.

- Add the salmon, prawns, mussels and half of the thyme, then add the wine and bring to a simmer before covering with the stock.

- Cover with a lid and cook at a simmer for 3–4 minutes, then spoon the mixture into a round baking dish. Pick out the mussel meat from the shells and discard the shells.

- Preheat the oven to 190°C (170°C fan) / 375F / gas 5.

- Roll out the pastry on a lightly floured surface into a round approximately 1 cm (½ in) thick.

- Drape over the baking dish and seal against the rim of the dish, then cut away the excess.

- Brush with the beaten egg. Bake for 20–25 minutes until puffed and golden. Serve with more thyme as a garnish.

SERVES 4

PREPARATION TIME 20 MINUTES

COOKING TIME 35–45 MINUTES

INGREDIENTS

2 tbsp olive oil

½ large leek, sliced

salt and freshly ground black pepper

450 g / 1 lb / 3 cups skinless salmon fillet, diced

300 g / 10 ½ oz / 2 cups whole prawns (shrimp), peeled and deveined

150 g / 5 oz / 1 cup mussels, cleaned with beards removed

a small bunch of thyme sprigs

125 ml / 4 ½ fl. oz / ½ cup dry white wine

500 ml / 18 fl. oz / 2 cups fish stock

150 g / 5 oz prepared puff pastry

a little plain (all-purpose) flour, for dusting

1 small egg, beaten

TOP TIP

Rinse the leeks in a couple of changes of water to get rid of any dirt or grit.

Haddock Potato-topped Pie

SERVES 4

PREPARATION TIME 25 MINUTES

COOKING TIME 1 HOUR 5–10 MINUTES

INGREDIENTS

- 1 kg / 2 lb 4 oz / 6 ⅔ cups floury potatoes, peeled and diced
- 75 g / 3 ½ oz / ⅓ cup butter
- 750 ml / 18 fl. oz / 3 cups whole (full-fat) milk
- Salt and freshly ground black pepper
- 600 g / 1 lb 5 oz / 4 cups haddock fillet
- 1 bay leaf
- 1 tsp black peppercorns
- A few sprigs of tarragon, chopped

METHOD

- Cook the potatoes in a large saucepan of salted, boiling water for 15–20 minutes until tender to the point of a knife.

- Drain and leave to cool for a few minutes, then mash with the butter, 4 tbsp of milk and some seasoning. Cover and set to one side.

- Place the haddock fillet in a large saucepan and cover with the remaining milk, the bay leaf and the peppercorns.

- Bring to a simmer over a medium heat. Cook at a steady simmer for 4–5 minutes until firm and slightly opaque in appearance.

- Strain the mixture, discarding the bay leaf and peppercorns but reserving the liquid. Preheat the oven to 180°C (160°C fan) / 350F / gas 4.

- Spoon the haddock and some of the liquid into the base of a heatproof baking dish. Top with the tarragon and smooth over the mashed potato.

- Bake the pie for 35–40 minutes until golden on top, then serve.

TOP TIP
Lightly crush the peppercorns to extract as much taste as possible.

Haddock, Cod and Prawn Pie

SERVES 6
PREPARATION TIME 15–20 MINUTES
COOKING TIME 1 HOUR 5–15 MINUTES

INGREDIENTS

1 kg / 2 lb 4 oz / 6 ⅔ cups floury potatoes, peeled and diced

110 g / 4 oz / ½ cup unsalted butter

1 tbsp sunflower oil

2 large carrots, peeled and sliced

4 sticks of celery, sliced

1 courgette (zucchini), finely diced

salt and freshly ground black pepper

450 g / 1 lb / 3 cups haddock fillet, cut into chunks

300 g / 10 ½ oz / 2 cups cod fillet, cut into chunks

300 g / 10 ½ oz / 2 cups prawns (shrimp), peeled and de-veined

500 ml / 18 fl. oz / 2 cups fish stock

150 g / 5 oz / 1 ½ cups Cheddar, grated

METHOD

- Cook the potato in a large saucepan of salted, boiling water for 15–20 minutes until tender to the point of a knife.

- Drain well and leave to cool slightly, then mash with 75 g / 2 ½ oz / ⅓ cup of the butter and some seasoning.

- Melt the rest of the butter with the oil in a large saucepan. Add the carrot, celery, courgette and a little salt and sweat for 7–8 minutes until softened.

- Add the fish, prawns and stock. Bring to a simmer and cook uncovered for 5 minutes.

- Preheat the oven to 180°C (160°C fan) / 350F / gas 4.

- Spoon the vegetables, fish and seafood into a large, oval baking dish.

- Top with the mashed potato and Cheddar and bake for 35–45 minutes until golden brown on top, then serve.

TOP TIP

Let the fish pie stand for 5–10 minutes before serving.

Shellfish Pie

SERVES 4

PREPARATION TIME 15 MINUTES

COOKING TIME 45–50 MINUTES

INGREDIENTS

2 tbsp unsalted butter

2 tbsp plain (all-purpose) flour, plus extra
for dusting

750 ml / 1 pint 6 fl. oz / 3 cups whole (full-fat)
milk

300 g / 10 ½ oz / 2 cups prawns (shrimp),
peeled and de-veined

225 g / 8 oz / 1 ½ cups mussels, cleaned,
with beards removed

300 g / 10 ½ oz / 2 cups haddock fillet,
cut into chunks

salt and freshly ground black pepper

a small bunch of flat-leaf parsley,
finely chopped

2 tbsp olive oil

300 g / 10 ½ oz prepared puff pastry

1 large egg, beaten

METHOD

- Melt the butter in a large saucepan
  set over a medium heat until hot.
  Add the flour and whisk until you
  have a smooth roux.

- Whisk in the milk in a slow, steady
  stream until smooth and slightly
  thickened.

- Bring to a simmer and cook for
  2 minutes, then add the prawns,
  mussels and haddock. Cover with a
  lid and cook for 3 minutes.

- Discard any mussels that haven't
  opened. Pick the meat from the shells
  and discard the shells.

- Season the shellfish filling and stir
  through the parsley. Spoon into
  4 individual baking dishes and
  drizzle with olive oil, then place on a
  baking tray.

- Preheat the oven to 180°C (160°C
  fan) / 350F / gas 4.

- Roll out the pastry on a lightly
  floured surface to 1 cm (½ in)
  thickness and cut out 4 rounds to
  cover the tops of the dishes.

- Drape over the dishes and seal well
  against their rims, cutting away any
  excess. Brush with the beaten egg
  and bake for 20–25 minutes until
  golden and puffed, then serve.

Smoked Trout Pie

SERVES 6

PREPARATION TIME 15–20 MINUTES

COOKING TIME 1 HOUR 5–15 MINUTES

INGREDIENTS

1 kg / 2 lb 4 oz / 6 ⅔ cups floury potatoes, peeled and diced

110 g / 4 oz / ½ cup unsalted butter

salt and freshly ground black pepper

2 shallots, finely chopped

150 g / 5 oz / 2 cups chestnut mushrooms, finely chopped

750 g / 1 lb 10 oz / 5 cups smoked trout fillet

125 ml / 4 ½ fl. oz / ½ cup dry white wine

250 ml / 9 fl. oz / 1 cup fish stock

75 g / 3 oz / ¾ cup dry breadcrumbs

METHOD

- Cook the potatoes in a large saucepan of salted, boiling water for 15–20 minutes until tender to the point of a knife.

- Drain well and leave to cool for a few minutes, then mash with 75 g / 2 ½ oz / ⅓ cup of butter and some seasoning.

- Melt the rest of the butter in a large saucepan set over a medium heat until hot.

- Add the shallot, mushrooms and a little salt and sweat for 6–7 minutes until softened.

- Add the trout and cover with the wine and stock. Bring to a simmer and cook uncovered for 5 minutes, then season to taste.

- Preheat the oven to 180°C (160°C fan) / 350F / gas 4.

- Spoon the trout mixture into the base of an oval baking dish and top with the mashed potato and breadcrumbs.

- Bake for 35–40 minutes until golden on top, then serve.

TOP TIP

Pick through the trout for any bones or cartilage before cooking.

Individual Fish Pie

SERVES 4

PREPARATION TIME 30 MINUTES

COOKING TIME 1 HOUR 30–40 MINUTES

INGREDIENTS

450 g / 1 lb prepared suet pastry

a little plain (all-purpose) flour, for dusting

750 g / 1 lb 10 oz / 5 cups salmon fillet, diced

150 ml / 5 fl. oz / ⅔ cup dry white wine

1 bouquet garni

4 large eggs

salt and freshly ground black pepper

a few chives, finely chopped

2 large egg yolks, beaten

METHOD

- Preheat the oven to 160°C (140°C fan) / 325F / gas 3. Roll out two-thirds of the pastry on a lightly floured surface to ½ cm (¼ in) thickness and use it to line 4 individual pie moulds.

- Press well into the base and sides, then trim any excess pastry and chill until needed.

- Place the salmon in a large saucepan and cover with the wine and enough water to submerge, then add the bouquet garni and bring to a simmer over a medium heat.

- Cook for 6–8 minutes until the fish is firm and cooked, then drain the liquid and discard the bouquet garni.

- Flake the fish into a bowl. Cook the eggs in a large saucepan of boiling water for 12 minutes.

- Drain the eggs and refresh in iced water, then peel and chop and add them to the salmon. Season with salt and pepper and stir in the chives.

- Spoon the mixture into the lined pastries. Roll out the remaining pastry to ½ cm (¼ in) thickness and cut out 4 rounds.

- Drape over the filling and seal against the side of the lined pastry. Brush the tops with egg yolk and bake for 50–60 minutes until the pastry is cooked through, then serve.

Anchovy Pie

SERVES 6

PREPARATION TIME 10 MINUTES

COOKING TIME 1 HOUR 10–20 MINUTES

INGREDIENTS

400 g / 14 oz prepared hot water pastry

a little plain (all-purpose) flour, for dusting

225 g / 8 oz / 1 ½ cups canned anchovy fillets, drained

350 g / 12 oz / 3 cups halloumi, sliced

1 lemon, juiced

salt and freshly ground black pepper

1 large egg, beaten

METHOD

- Preheat the oven to 160°C (140°C fan) / 325F / gas 3. Roll out two-thirds of the pastry on a lightly floured surface to 1 cm (½ in) thickness and use it to line a 18 cm (7 in) springform cake tin.

- Press well into the base and sides, trimming away any excess, then cover and chill.

- Toss the anchovy fillets with the halloumi, lemon juice and seasoning in a mixing bowl.

- Arrange the halloumi slices and anchovy fillets in the lined pastry. Roll out the remaining pastry on a lightly floured surface to 1 cm (½ in) thickness.

- Drape the pastry over the anchovy filling. Seal well against the side of the lined pastry, then trim the excess.

- Brush the top with beaten egg and bore a small hole in the middle. Bake for 1 hour 10–20 minutes until the pastry is golden and cooked.

- Remove to a wire rack to cool before turning out and serving.

TOP TIP
Take into account the saltiness of the cheese and anchovies when seasoning.

Vegetable Pies

Cheese and Onion Pie

SERVES 4

PREPARATION TIME 20 MINUTES

COOKING TIME 1 HOUR

INGREDIENTS

3 tbsp unsalted butter

2 onions, finely sliced

salt and freshly ground black pepper

150 g / 5 oz / 3 cups baby spinach, washed

150 g / 5 oz / 1 ½ cups Cheddar, grated

3 large eggs, beaten

110 ml / 4 fl. oz / ½ cup whole (full-fat) milk

200 g / 7 oz prepared shortcrust pastry

a little plain (all-purpose) flour, for dusting

METHOD

- Preheat the oven to 180°C (160°C fan) / 350F / gas 4. Melt the butter in a large saucepan set over a medium heat until hot.

- Add the onion and a little salt and sweat for 7–8 minutes until softened, then add the spinach.

- Cook for 3–4 minutes until wilted, then strain the spinach and onions through a colander to extract as much water as possible.

- Roughly chop and move to a large mixing bowl. Add the cheese and eggs, stirring well.

- Roll out the pastry on a lightly floured surface into a large round approximately 1 cm (½ in) thick.

- Drape over a 20 cm (8 in) tart tin, pressing well into the base and sides. Cut away any excess overhanging pastry and prick the base with a fork.

- Fill with the cheese and onion mixture and bake for 35–45 minutes until the pastry is golden and cooked.

- Remove to a wire rack to cool before turning out and serving.

TOP TIP

Extract as much water as possible from the spinach before adding to the pie.

Pumpkin Pie

MAKES 4

PREPARATION TIME 20 MINUTES

COOKING TIME 45–55 MINUTES

INGREDIENTS

500 g / 1 lb 5 oz / 4 cups pumpkin, peeled and diced

300 g / 10 ½ oz / 2 cups floury potatoes, peeled and diced

100 g / 3 ½ oz / ½ cup butter

75 ml / 3 fl. oz / ⅓ cup whole (full-fat) milk

a pinch of ground nutmeg

salt and freshly ground black pepper

250 g / 9 oz prepared puff pastry

a little plain (all-purpose) flour, for dusting

1 large egg, beaten

METHOD

- Cook the pumpkin and potato in a large saucepan of salted, boiling water for 15–20 minutes until tender to the point of a knife.

- Drain well and leave to cool slightly, then mash with the butter, milk, nutmeg and seasoning. Spoon into the base of 4 individual baking dishes.

- Preheat the oven to 190°C (170°C fan) / 375F / gas 5.

- Roll out the pastry on a lightly floured surface into a large round approximately ½ cm (¼ in) thick. Use a sharp knife or large cookie cutter to cut out 4 rounds to top the dishes.

- Drape the pastry rounds over the dishes and seal against the rims, using a little beaten egg if necessary.

- Place on a large baking tray and brush their tops with more beaten egg.

- Bake for 20–25 minutes until the pastry is golden and puffed, then serve.

TOP TIP
Serve these pies fresh from the oven before the pastry lids deflate.

Greek Feta and Spinach Pie

SERVES 6

PREPARATION TIME 20 MINUTES

COOKING TIME 55–60 MINUTES

INGREDIENTS

3 tbsp olive oil

1 onion, finely chopped

1 red onion, finely chopped

½ tsp dried oregano

½ tsp dried thyme

300 g / 10 ½ oz / 6 cups baby spinach, washed

400 g / 14 oz / 2 ½ cups ricotta

200 g / 7 oz / 2 cups feta, crumbled

salt and freshly ground black pepper

4 sheets of filo pastry, kept under a damp
   towel

3 tbsp unsalted butter, melted

METHOD

- Preheat the oven to 190°C (170°C fan) / 375F / gas 5 and line the base and sides of a 20 cm (8 in) springform cake tin with a sheet of greaseproof paper.

- Heat the oil in a large saucepan set over a moderate heat until hot. Sauté the onions for 4–5 minutes, stirring frequently, until golden.

- Add the herbs and the spinach and let the spinach wilt over a reduced heat before removing from the heat.

- Drain the spinach and onions through a colander, then roughly chop and place in a mixing bowl.

- Add the ricotta and feta; mix well with your hands and season to taste.

- Line the prepared tin with 2 sheets of filo pastry, then spoon the filling on top, smoothing with the back of a spoon.

- Drape the remaining filo sheets on top, tucking the edges over and in, then brush the top with melted butter.

- Bake for 35–45 minutes until golden on top. Remove from the oven and leave to cool a little before turning out and serving.

Paprika Pie

SERVES 4

PREPARATION TIME 15–20 MINUTES

COOKING TIME 50–60 MINUTES

INGREDIENTS

2 tbsp sunflower oil

1 onion, finely sliced

2 cloves of garlic, chopped

salt and freshly ground black pepper

1 medium head of cauliflower, cut into florets

225 g / 8 oz / 1 ½ cups baby potatoes, halved

1 tsp smoked paprika

1 tsp sweet paprika

350 g / 12 oz prepared puff pastry

a little plain (all-purpose) flour, for dusting

1 large egg yolk, beaten

METHOD

- Preheat the oven to 180°C (160°C fan) / 350F / gas 4 and heat the oil in a casserole dish set over a medium heat until hot.

- Add the onion, garlic and a little salt and sweat for 4–5 minutes until softened.

- Stir in the cauliflower, baby potatoes and paprika, then cover the dish with a lid and cook over a very low heat for 7–8 minutes, stirring occasionally.

- Roll out two-thirds of the pastry on a lightly floured surface to ½ cm (¼ in) thickness and use to line a round baking dish.

- Trim away the excess before filling with the cauliflower and potato mixture. Roll out the remaining pastry to the same thickness as before and drape over the baking dish.

- Seal well against the lined pastry and cut away the excess. Gather and reroll the excess and cut into strips.

- Brush the top with beaten egg, then decorate with the strips of pastry. Bake for 30–40 minutes until puffed and golden, then serve.

TOP TIP

Grease the baking dish with a little oil before lining with the pastry.

Mushroom and Potato Pie

MAKES 4

PREPARATION TIME 15 MINUTES

COOKING TIME 45 MINUTES

INGREDIENTS

3 tbsp unsalted butter

2 shallots, finely chopped

2 cloves of garlic, minced

salt and freshly ground black pepper

150 g / 5 oz / 2 cups closed cup mushrooms, roughly chopped

150 g / 5 oz / 2 cups chestnut mushrooms, roughly chopped

75 g / 3 oz / 1 cup chanterelles, chopped

450 g / 1 lb / 3 cups floury potatoes, peeled and diced

a small bunch of flat-leaf parsley, chopped

250 g / 9 oz prepared shortcrust pastry

a little plain (all-purpose) flour, for dusting

1 large egg, beaten

METHOD

- Melt the butter in a large saucepan set over a medium heat until hot. Add the shallot, garlic and a little salt and sweat for 4–5 minutes.

- Add the mushrooms and potato and continue to cook for 8–10 minutes, stirring occasionally, until softened.

- Stir through the parsley and adjust the seasoning to taste, then spoon into the base of 4 individual ovenproof mugs.

- Preheat the oven to 180°C (160°C fan) / 350F / gas 4.

- Roll out the pastry on a lightly floured surface to 1 cm (½ in) thickness and cut 4 rounds that will act as lids for the pies.

- Wet the rims of the mugs with a little water, then drape the pastry lids over them. Seal the lids against the rim using your thumb and forefinger.

- Score a pattern on top of the pastry with a sharp knife and brush with the beaten egg.

- Arrange on a baking tray and bake for 20–25 minutes until golden brown and cooked before serving.

TOP TIP
The potato and mushrooms will need plenty of seasoning.

Broccoli and Cauliflower Pie

SERVES 4

PREPARATION TIME 15 MINUTES

COOKING TIME 40–45 MINUTES

INGREDIENTS

- tbsp olive oil
- tbsp unsalted butter
- medium onions, chopped
- medium courgettes (zucchinis), finely diced
- medium carrots, peeled and diced
- salt and freshly ground black pepper
- head of broccoli, prepared into small florets
- small head of cauliflower, prepared into small florets
- 50 g / 5 oz prepared shortcrust pastry
- little plain (all-purpose) flour, for dusting
- small egg, beaten
- tbsp white sesame seeds

METHOD

- Preheat the oven to 180°C (160°C fan) / 350F / gas 4. Heat the oil and butter together in a large saucepan set over a medium heat until hot.

- Sweat the onion, courgette and carrot with a little salt for 5 minutes, stirring occasionally.

- Add the broccoli and cauliflower and continue to cook over a reduced heat for 3–4 minutes until tender, then spoon into a round pie dish.

- Roll out the pastry into a 1 cm (½ in) thick round on a lightly floured surface. Drape over the dish, cutting away any excess from the rim.

- Brush with beaten egg and top with sesame seeds, then bake for 25–30 minutes until golden brown at the edges.

- Remove from the oven and leave to cool for 5 minutes before serving.

TOP TIP

Use the baking dish as a guide for rolling out the pastry to the correct size.

VEGETABLE PIES

Cheese and Potato Pie

SERVES 4

PREPARATION TIME 20 MINUTES

COOKING TIME 1 HOUR 10–20 MINUTES

INGREDIENTS

150 ml / 5 fl. oz / ⅔ cup whole (full-fat) milk

150 ml / 5 fl. oz / ⅔ cup double (heavy) cream

2 cloves of garlic, minced

750 g / 1 lb 10 oz / 5 cups floury potatoes,
    peeled and sliced

350 g / 12 oz prepared shortcrust pastry

a little plain (all-purpose) flour, for dusting

150 g / 5 oz / 1 ½ cups reblochon, cubed

150 g / 5 oz / 1 ½ cups Cheddar, grated

salt and freshly ground black pepper

1 large egg, beaten

100 g / 3 ½ oz / 2 cups baby spinach, washed

a few sprigs of dill

METHOD

- Combine the milk, cream and garlic in a saucepan and warm over a medium heat until simmering.

- Add the potato slices and stir well before covering with a lid. Cook over a reduced heat for 5 minutes, then remove from the heat.

- Preheat the oven to 160°C (140°C fan) / 325F / gas 3.

- Roll out two-thirds of the pastry on a lightly floured surface to 1 cm (½ in) thickness and use it to line the base and sides of a 20 cm (8 in) square baking dish.

- Prick the base with a fork, then top with the potato and cream mixture. Sprinkle over the cheeses and some seasoning, then stir briefly to mix.

- Roll out the remaining pastry into a square approximately 1 cm (½ in) thick. Drape over the filling and seal against the edge of the other pastry by crimping between thumb and forefinger.

- Brush with beaten egg, then bake for 45–50 minutes until the pastry is golden and cooked. Serve with baby spinach and dill on the side.

TOP TIP
This pie can be made in advance and served cold.

Forest Mushroom Pie

SERVES 4

PREPARATION TIME 15 MINUTES

COOKING TIME 1 HOUR 10–20 MINUTES

INGREDIENTS

3 tbsp unsalted butter

2 shallots, finely chopped

2 cloves of garlic, minced

450 g / 1 lb / 3 cups mixed wild mushrooms, sliced

a small bunch of flat-leaf parsley, finely chopped

½ lemon, juiced

salt and freshly ground black pepper

400 g / 14 oz prepared hot water pastry

a little plain (all-purpose) flour, for dusting

1 large egg, beaten

METHOD

- Melt the butter in a large saucepan set over a medium heat until hot. Add the shallot, garlic and a little salt and sweat for 5–6 minutes.

- Add the mushrooms and continue to cook for 5–6 minutes, stirring occasionally.

- Stir through the parsley and lemon juice and season to taste, then set to one side to cool.

- Preheat the oven to 160°C (140°C fan) / 325F / gas 3. Roll out two-thirds of the pastry on a lightly floured surface into a large round approximately 1 cm (½ in) thick.

- Use the pastry round to line the base and sides of a large, round baking dish; let the excess pastry overhang by 5 cm (2 in).

- Fill with the mushroom mixture. Roll out the remaining pastry into a round the same diameter as the baking dish, approximately 1 cm (½ in) thick.

- Lay the pastry round on top of the mushrooms, bringing the excess overhanging pastry back over the rim and over the pastry and pleating to seal.

- Brush with beaten egg and bore a small hole in the middle. Bake for 50–60 minutes until golden and cooked before serving.

Spinach and Goats' Cheese Pie

SERVES 4

PREPARATION TIME 15 MINUTES

COOKING TIME 55–60 MINUTES

INGREDIENTS

3 tbsp olive oil

2 onions, finely chopped

1 tsp dried oregano

½ tsp dried basil

450 g / 1 lb oz / 9 cups baby spinach, washed

300 g / 10 ½ oz / 3 cups goats' cheese, crumbled

salt and freshly ground black pepper

4 large sheets of filo pastry, kept under a damp towel

3 tbsp unsalted butter, melted

METHOD

- Preheat the oven to 180°C (160°C fan) / 350F / gas 4.

- Heat the oil in a large saucepan set over a moderate heat until hot, then sweat the onions for 5–6 minutes.

- Add the herbs and the spinach. Let the spinach wilt over a reduced heat before removing from the heat.

- Drain the spinach and onions through a colander, then roughly chop and place in a mixing bowl.

- Add half of the crumbled goats' cheese and mix well, then season to taste.

- Line an 18 cm (7 in) springform cake tin with the sheets of pastry, brushing melted butter between each one; let the pastry overhang the rim.

- Spoon the filling on top, smoothing with the back of a spoon, then top with the rest of the goats' cheese. Bring the overhanging pastry back over the filling, folding to fit.

- Bake for 35–40 minutes until cooked through. Remove from the oven and leave to cool a little before turning out and serving.

TOP TIP

The pie can be finished under a hot grill to brown the top.

Curried Vegetable Pie

ERVES 4

REPARATION TIME 15 MINUTES

OOKING TIME 1 HOUR 5–15 MINUTES

INGREDIENTS

- 0 g / 1 lb 5 oz / 4 cups new potatoes
- bsp unsalted butter
- onion, finely sliced
- cloves of garlic, minced
- lt and freshly ground black pepper
- yellow courgette (zucchini), sliced
- sp Madras curry powder
- pinch of Cayenne pepper
- 0 ml / 9 fl. oz / 1 cup double (heavy) cream
- 0 g / 12 oz prepared puff pastry
- ittle plain (all-purpose) flour, for dusting
- arge egg, beaten

METHOD

- Cook the potatoes in a large saucepan of salted, boiling water for 15–20 minutes until tender to the point of a knife.

- Drain well and leave to cool briefly, then slice. Melt the butter in a large saucepan set over a medium heat until hot.

- Add the onion, garlic and a little salt. Sweat for 5–6 minutes until softened, then add the courgette. Continue to cook for 2 minutes, then stir in the curry powder and Cayenne.

- Pour in the cream, bring to a simmer, and cover with a lid. Cook over a low heat for 5 minutes, then season to taste.

- Preheat the oven to 180°C (160°C fan) / 350F / gas 4. Roll out two-thirds of the pastry on a lightly floured surface into a 1 cm (½ in) thick round.

- Use the pastry to line a 20 cm (8 in) round baking dish. Cut away any excess overhanging pastry and prick the base with a fork.

- Fill with the vegetable filling, then roll out the remaining pastry into a 1 cm (½ in) round. Drape over the filling and seal against the other pastry using your thumb and forefinger.

- Brush with beaten egg and bore a hole in the middle. Bake for 25–30 minutes until golden and puffed, then serve.

Aubergine Pie

SERVES 4–6

PREPARATION TIME 25 MINUTES

COOKING TIME 35–45 MINUTES

INGREDIENTS

350 g / 12 oz prepared puff pastry

a little plain (all-purpose) flour, for dusting

110 ml / 4 fl. oz / ½ cup extra virgin olive oil

1 tsp dried oregano

2 aubergines (eggplants), sliced into thin strips

1 red onion, finely sliced

1 courgette (zucchini), sliced into thin strips

2 cloves of garlic, minced

salt and freshly ground black pepper

1 large egg, beaten

a large handful of rocket (arugula), to serve

2 vine tomatoes, cored and finely diced

METHOD

- Preheat the oven to 160°C (140°C fan) / 325F / gas 3. Grease and line a large baking tray with a sheet of greaseproof paper.

- Roll out the pastry on a lightly floured surface into a large rectangle approximately 60 cm x 40 cm (24 in x 16 in) and 1 cm (½ in) thick.

- Cut in half down the middle so that you have two identical pieces of pastry. Reserve any leftover pastry, reroll to 1 cm (½ in) thickness and cut into decorative shapes.

- Lift one piece of the pastry onto the lined baking tray. Mix the olive oil with the oregano and toss half with the vegetables, garlic and plenty of seasoning in a mixing bowl.

- Spoon the mixture onto the pastry on the baking tray, leaving a 2 cm (1 in) border all the way around. Brush the border with some beaten egg, then lift the other piece of pastry on top of the filling.

- Seal the pastries together using your fingers. Brush the top with more beaten egg, then decorate with the pastry shapes and brush again with more egg.

- Bake for 35–45 minutes until golden and puffed. Serve with a rocket and tomato salad and the remaining olive oil and oregano as a dressing.

Savoury Tarts and Pastries

Quiche Lorraine

SERVES 6

PREPARATION TIME 10 MINUTES

COOKING TIME 1 HOUR 10 MINUTES

INGREDIENTS

250 g / 9 oz prepared shortcrust pastry

a little plain (all-purpose) flour, for dusting

2 tbsp unsalted butter

100 g / 3 ½ oz / ⅔ cup pancetta, diced

375 ml / 13 fl. oz / 1 ½ cups whole (full-fat) milk

250 g / 9 oz / 1 cup crème fraiche

5 large eggs

150 g / 5 oz / 1 ½ cups Gruyère, grated

salt and freshly ground black pepper

150 g / 5 oz / 3 cups mixed leaf salad, to serve

75 g / 3 oz / ½ cup cherry tomatoes, halved

METHOD

- Preheat the oven to 160°C (140°C fan) / 325F / gas 3.

- Roll out the pastry on a floured surface to 1 cm (½ in) thickness and use it to line a 18 cm (7 in) tart tin. Prick the base with a fork and chill.

- Melt the butter in a saucepan set over a moderate heat until hot.

- Add the pancetta and fry for 2–3 minutes until golden, then drain on kitchen paper.

- Whisk together the milk, crème fraiche, eggs, Gruyère and seasoning until thoroughly incorporated.

- Arrange the pancetta in the base of the pastry, then pour over the egg filling. Bake for 50–60 minutes until the filling is set and the pastry is cooked.

- Remove to a wire rack to cool before turning out and serving with salad and cherry tomatoes on the side.

TOP TIP

If the filling is set but slightly wobbly to the touch, it is perfectly cooked.

Cornish Pasty

MAKES 4

PREPARATION TIME 25 MINUTES

COOKING TIME 55–60 MINUTES

INGREDIENTS

2 tbsp unsalted butter

1 large onion, finely chopped

2 small white potatoes, peeled and finely
    diced

½ turnip, peeled and finely diced

salt and freshly ground black pepper

450 g / 1 lb / 3 cups steak mince

250 ml / 9 fl. oz / 1 cup beef stock

a few dashes of Worcestershire sauce

250 g / 12 oz prepared shortcrust pastry

a little plain (all-purpose) flour, for dusting

1 large egg, beaten

METHOD

- Melt the butter in a large casserole dish set over a medium heat until hot. Add the onion, potato, turnip and salt and sweat for 8–10 minutes until softened.

- Add the steak mince and cook for 4–5 minutes until browned.

- Cover with the stock and Worcestershire sauce, then stir well and simmer for 8–10 minutes until most of the liquid has evaporated. Season to taste.

- Preheat the oven to 180°C (160°C fan) / 350F / gas 4.

- Roll out the pastry on a lightly floured surface to 1 cm (½ in) thickness. Cut out 12 cm (5 in) rounds using a straight-sided cookie cutter.

- Fill the centre of the rounds with the beef filling, then wet the edges with a little water.

- Bring the edges of the pastry over the filling to meet above the centre. Seal by crimping between thumb and forefinger and then arrange on a baking tray.

- Brush the pastries with the beaten egg. Bake for 30 minutes until golden brown and cooked through. Serve either hot or cool.

Spinach and Feta Pastries

MAKES 4

PREPARATION TIME 25 MINUTES

COOKING TIME 20 MINUTES

INGREDIENTS

3 tbsp olive oil

300 g / 10 ½ oz / 6 cups baby spinach, washed

150 g / 5 oz / 1 ½ cups feta cheese, cubed

salt and freshly ground black pepper

250 g / 9 oz prepared shortcrust pastry

a little plain (all-purpose) flour, for dusting

1 large egg, beaten

METHOD

- Preheat the oven to 190°C (170°C fan) / 375F / gas 5 and line a baking tray with greaseproof paper.

- Heat the olive oil in a large frying pan set over a moderate heat until hot, then wilt the spinach in the hot oil until soft.

- Reduce the heat slightly before stirring in the feta. Season to taste, then press the spinach against a colander to extract some water.

- Roll out the pastry on a lightly floured surface into a large round approximately ½ cm (¼ in) thick. Use a 10 cm (4 in) cookie cutter to cut out rounds of pastry.

- Place 1 tbsp of the spinach filling in the centre of each round of pastry; wet the rim with a little water.

- Fold the pastry over the filling to form a semi-circle, making sure to seal the edges well. Arrange on a baking tray and brush the tops with beaten egg.

- Bake for 14–16 minutes until golden and puffed, then serve.

TOP TIP

For a shinier glaze, beat the egg yolk with 1 tbsp of milk before brushing on the pastries.

Goats' Cheese and Leek Tart

SERVES 4–6

PREPARATION TIME 15 MINUTES

COOKING TIME 1 HOUR 15–25 MINUTES

INGREDIENTS

600 g / 1 lb 5 oz / 4 cups floury potatoes, peeled and diced

75 g / 3 oz / ⅓ cup crème fraiche

salt and freshly ground black pepper

200 g / 7 oz / 2 cups goats' cheese, crumbled

2 tbsp unsalted butter

1 large leek, sliced

250 g / 9 oz prepared shortcrust pastry

a little plain (all-purpose) flour, for dusting

METHOD

- Cook the potato in a large saucepan of salted, boiling water for 15–20 minutes until tender to the point of a knife. Drain well and leave to cool slightly.

- Mash the potato with the crème fraiche and seasoning until smooth, then add the goats' cheese and mash again briefly to incorporate.

- Preheat the oven to 160°C (140°C fan) / 325F / gas 3.

- Melt the butter in a large frying pan set over a medium heat until hot. Add the leek and a little salt and sweat for 5–6 minutes until softened, then set to one side.

- Roll out the pastry on a lightly floured surface into a round approximately 2 cm (1 in) thick. Line a cast-iron pan with the round of pastry, creating a rough border around the rim.

- Prick the pastry all over with a fork and fill with the potato and cheese filling. Smooth with the back of a spoon, then scatter over half of the sweated leek.

- Bake for 50–60 minutes until the pastry is cooked through. Serve with the rest of the leek as a garnish on top.

Turkey Pastries

MAKES 8

PREPARATION TIME 25 MINUTES

COOKING TIME 40 MINUTES

INGREDIENTS

2 tbsp unsalted butter

1 tbsp sunflower oil

1 onion, finely chopped

450 g / 1 lb / 3 cups turkey leg meat, diced

150 g / 5 oz / 2 cups fresh breadcrumbs

salt and freshly ground black pepper

400 g / 14 oz prepared puff pastry

a little plain (all-purpose) flour, for dusting

2 large egg yolks, beaten with 1 tbsp water

2 tbsp black sesame seeds

METHOD

- Preheat the oven to 190°C (170°C fan) / 375F / gas 5. Melt the butter with the oil in a large sauté pan set over a moderate heat until hot.

- Add the onion and sauté for 3–4 minutes, then add the turkey and cook for 6–7 minutes until browned.

- Remove the pan from the heat and stir through the breadcrumbs and seasoning to taste.

- Divide the pastry in half and roll out each piece on a lightly floured surface into large rectangles that are ½ cm (¼ in) thick.

- Use a sharp knife to cut out 8 rectangles of pastry, 10 cm x 5 cm (4 in x 2 in) in dimension from each piece, giving you 16 rectangles of pastry.

- Spoon the turkey filling down the middle of half of the rectangles, leaving a small border all the way around.

- Wet the border with some water before lifting the other pastry rectangles on top; seal the pastries together.

- Arrange on a large baking tray and brush the tops with the egg yolk glaze. Sprinkle over some sesame seeds and bake for 18–22 minutes until golden before serving.

Cheese and Tomato Tarts

SERVES 4–6

PREPARATION TIME 10–15 MINUTES

COOKING TIME 30–35 MINUTES

INGREDIENTS

300 g / 10 ½ oz prepared shortcrust pastry

a little plain (all-purpose) flour, for dusting

2 large egg yolks

2 large eggs

250 g / 9 oz / 1 cup crème fraiche

300 g / 10 ½ oz / 3 cups Cheddar, grated

salt and freshly ground black pepper

6 vine tomatoes, cored and halved

a small bunch of sage, leaves picked

a small handful of flat-leaf parsley, finely chopped

2 tbsp extra virgin olive oil

2 tbsp balsamic vinegar

METHOD

- Preheat the oven to 190°C (170°C fan) / 375F / gas 5.

- Roll out the pastry on a lightly floured surface into a large rectangle approximately ½ cm (¼ in) thick.

- Use the pastry to line the base and sides of a shallow rectangular tart tin, then prick the base with a fork and chill.

- Whisk together the egg yolks, eggs, crème fraiche, Cheddar and seasoning. Spoon over the pastry and top with the tomato halves, cut-side facing up.

- Sprinkle over the sage and parsley, then drizzle over the olive oil and vinegar.

- Bake for 30–35 minutes until the pastry is cooked and the filling is set.

- Remove to a wire rack to cool before turning out and serving.

TOP TIP

This tart can also be browned under a hot grill just before slicing and serving.

131

Pea and Parmesan Pastries

MAKES 4

PREPARATION TIME 20 MINUTES

COOKING TIME 35–45 MINUTES

INGREDIENTS

300 g / 10 ½ oz prepared shortcrust pastry
a little plain (all-purpose) flour, for dusting
150 g / 5 oz / ⅔ cup crème fraiche
150 ml / 5 fl. oz / ⅔ cup whole (full-fat) milk
4 large eggs
150 g / 5 oz / 1 ½ cups Parmesan, grated
110 g / 4 oz / 1 cup peas
4 small tomatoes, cut into wedges
450 g / 1 lb / 3 cups baby carrots, halved
salt and freshly ground black pepper

METHOD

- Preheat the oven to 180°C (160°C fan) / 350F / gas 4.

- Roll out the pastry on a lightly floured surface to 1 cm (½ in) thickness and cut out 4 rounds of pastry to line the base and sides of 4 tartlet tins.

- Press the pastry into the base and sides of the tins, then cut away any excess pastry. Prick with a fork.

- Whisk together the crème fraiche, milk, eggs and Parmesan with a little seasoning. Stir through the peas and tomatoes, then spoon the mixture into the pastry cases.

- Arrange the carrots in patterns on top of the filling, then carefully move the tartlets to a baking tray.

- Bake for 35–45 minutes until the pastry is cooked through and the filling is set.

- Remove to a wire rack to cool before serving.

TOP TIP
Use your thumbs and index fingers to deftly line the cases with the pastry.

Leek, Bacon and Prawn Quiche

SERVES 6

PREPARATION TIME 15 MINUTES

COOKING TIME 55–60 MINUTES

INGREDIENTS

300 g / 10 ½ oz / 2 cups prawns (shrimp), peeled

2 tbsp unsalted butter

100 g / 3 ½ oz / ⅔ cup pancetta, diced

1 leek, sliced

3 large sheets of filo pastry

250 g / 9 oz / 1 cup crème fraiche

250 ml / 9 fl. oz / 1 cup double (heavy) cream

4 large eggs

150 g / 5 oz / 1 ½ cups Cheddar, grated

salt and freshly ground black pepper

1 lemon, thinly sliced

METHOD

- Preheat the oven to 180°C (160°C fan) / 350F / gas 4. Chop most of the prawns, saving 2 as a garnish.

- Melt the butter in a large sauté pan set over a medium heat until hot.

- Add the pancetta and leek and sweat for 6–8 minutes until the leek is soft, then tip into a mixing bowl.

- Line a 20 cm (8 in) fluted baking dish with the sheets of filo pastry. Add the crème fraiche, cream and eggs to the leek and pancetta.

- Whisk well before adding the cheese, chopped prawns and seasoning, whisking again briefly to incorporate.

- Pour into the lined baking dish and top with lemon slices, then bake for 40–45 minutes until the filling is set and the pastry is cooked.

- Remove to a wire rack to cool before turning out and serving.

TOP TIP
Grease the baking dish with a little oil to prevent the pastry from sticking.

Asparagus and Lemon Tart

SERVES 6

PREPARATION TIME 10 MINUTES

COOKING TIME 35–40 MINUTES

INGREDIENTS

250 g / 9 oz / 2 cups asparagus spears,
   woody ends removed

2 lemons

salt and freshly ground black pepper

3 sheets of filo pastry, kept under a damp
   towel

3 tbsp olive oil

150 g / 5 oz / 1 ½ cups grated mozzarella

55 g / 2 oz / ½ cup pine nuts

METHOD

- Preheat the oven to 190°C (170°C fan) / 375F / gas 5.

- Blanch the asparagus in a large saucepan of salted, boiling water for 2 minutes,then drain and refresh in iced water.

- Zest and juice the lemons into a mixing bowl. Add the asparagus and toss well before seasoning.

- Line a 20 cm (8 in) fluted pie dish with the sheets of filo pastry, brushing each with olive oil before lining.

- Sprinkle over the mozzarella, then top with the asparagus and pine nuts.

- Bake for 25–30 minutes until the pastry is golden before serving.

TOP TIP
You can peel the thicker asparagus spears so that they cook evenly.

Potato and Curry Samosas

MAKES 8

PREPARATION TIME 25 MINUTES

COOKING TIME 50–55 MINUTES

INGREDIENTS

750 g / 1 lb / 5 cups floury potatoes, peeled and finely diced

3 tbsp sunflower oil

1 large onion, finely chopped

2 cloves of garlic, minced

2 green chillies (chilis), deseeded and finely chopped

salt and freshly ground black pepper

1 tbsp Madras curry powder

2 tsp garam masala

350 g / 12 oz prepared shortcrust pastry

a little plain (all-purpose) flour, for dusting

250 g / 9 oz / 1 cup plain yoghurt

a small bunch of mint, finely chopped

METHOD

- Preheat the oven to 180°C (160°C fan) / 350F / gas 4. Cook the potato in a large saucepan of salted, boiling water for 6–8 minutes until tender to the point of a knife.

- Drain well and leave to cool to one side. Heat the oil in a large saucepan set over a medium heat until hot.

- Add the onion, garlic, chilli and a little salt. Sweat for 5–6 minutes until softened, then add the spices and stir well.

- Cook for 1 minute, then add the potato and stir again. Cook over a reduced heat for 2 minutes, then season to taste and set to one side.

- Roll out the pastry on a lightly floured surface into a large square approximately ½ cm (¼ in) thick and cut out 8 squares approximately 10 x 10 cm (4 x 4 in) in dimension.

- Spoon the curried potato filling into the centre of the squares. Wet the rims and fold one corner over to the other, crimping to seal.

- Arrange on a greaseproof paper-lined baking tray and prick with a fork a few times, then bake for 22–25 minutes until golden brown and cooked through.

- Stir together the yoghurt, mint and seasoning to serve with the samosas.

Tomato and Mozzarella Tarts

MAKES 4

PREPARATION TIME 20 MINUTES

COOKING TIME 20–25 MINUTES

INGREDIENTS

225 g / 8 oz prepared shortcrust pastry

a little plain (all-purpose) flour, for dusting

a large bunch of basil, leaves picked

2 cloves of garlic, chopped

75 g / 3 oz / ¾ cup Parmesan, chopped

110 ml / 4 fl. oz / ½ cup olive oil

salt and freshly ground black pepper

225 g / 8 oz / 1 cup sun-dried tomatoes in oil, drained

300 g / 10 ½ oz / 3 cups fresh mozzarella, drained and sliced

100 g / 3 ½ oz / ⅔ cup prosciutto slices

METHOD

- Preheat the oven to 180°C (160°C fan) / 350F / gas 4.

- Roll out the pastry on a lightly floured surface to ½ cm (¼ in) thickness. Cut out four 15 cm (6 in) rounds and use to line 4 individual fluted tartlet tins.

- Prick the bases with a fork and chill.

- Blend the basil leaves, garlic, Parmesan and oil in a food processor, then season to taste.

- Line the pastry cases with overlapping circles of sun-dried tomato and mozzarella. Top with the basil pesto and arrange the tins on a baking tray and bake the tarts for 20–25 minutes.

- Remove to a wire rack to cool, then serve with slices of prosciutto.

TOP TIP

Adjust the amount of oil in the pesto for a thicker or thinner sauce as desired.

Pear and Spinach Tart

SERVES 4

PREPARATION TIME 20 MINUTES

COOKING TIME 40–50 MINUTES

INGREDIENTS

250 g / 9 oz prepared shortcrust pastry

a little plain (all-purpose) flour, for dusting

2 tbsp olive oil

150 g / 5 oz / 3 cups baby spinach, washed

salt and freshly ground black pepper

110 g / 4 oz / 1 cup Cheddar, grated

1 large conference pear, cored and sliced

55 g / 2 oz / ½ cup pine nuts

a pinch of Cayenne pepper

METHOD

- Preheat the oven to 180°C (160°C fan) / 350F / gas 4.

- Roll out the pastry on a lightly floured surface into a rectangle approximately 1 cm (½ in) thick.

- Drape over a fluted rectangular tart tin. Press well into the base and sides and prick the base with a fork, then chill.

- Heat the olive oil in a large sauté pan set over a medium heat until hot. Add the spinach and some seasoning and cook until wilted.

- Drain the spinach through a colander and pat dry with kitchen paper, then spread over the base of the pastry.

- Top with the Cheddar, pear slices and pine nuts, then bake for 25–35 minutes until the pastry is cooked through and golden.

- Remove to a wire rack to cool before serving with a pinch of Cayenne pepper on top.

TOP TIP

When rolling out the pastry, apply even pressure and roll smoothly.

Ham and Cheese Turnovers

MAKES 8

PREPARATION TIME 25 MINUTES

COOKING TIME 30–35 MINUTES

INGREDIENTS

450 g / 1 lb prepared shortcrust pastry

a little plain (all-purpose) flour, for dusting

8 slices of ham

200 g / 7 oz / 2 cups mozzarella, sliced

2 large eggs, beaten

150 g / 5 oz / 1 cup sesame seeds

150 g / 5 oz / 1 ½ cups golden breadcrumbs

METHOD

- Preheat the oven to 180°C (160°C fan) / 350F / gas 4. Roll out the pastry on a lightly floured surface into a large round approximately 1 cm (½ in) thick.

- Cut out 8 ovals of pastry approximately 15 x 10 cm (6 x 4 in) in dimension.

- Cut the slices of ham to size and arrange on the pastry ovals, leaving a small border all the way around.

- Top with slices of mozzarella in the centre, then brush the borders with some beaten egg.

- Fold one edge over the filling and seal against the other using your fingers.

- Brush the sealed turnovers with more beaten egg, then dip in a mixture of the sesame seeds and breadcrumbs to coat.

- Arrange on a greaseproof paper-lined baking tray and bake for 30–35 minutes until cooked through, then serve.

TOP TIP

Don't forget to coat the undersides of the turnovers with sesame, as well as the tops.

Red Onion and Goats' Cheese Tart

SERVES 4–6

PREPARATION TIME 15 MINUTES

COOKING TIME 50–55 MINUTES

INGREDIENTS

2 tbsp unsalted butter

2 tbsp olive oil

2 large red onions, sliced

1 clove of garlic, minced

Salt and freshly ground black pepper

300 g / 10 ½ oz / 3 cups goats' cheese, crumbled

250 g / 9 oz prepared shortcrust pastry

A little plain (all-purpose) flour, for dusting

METHOD

- Preheat the oven to 180°C (160°C fan) / 350F / gas 4.

- Melt the butter with the oil in a frying or sauté pan set over a medium heat until hot.

- Add the onions, garlic and a little salt and sweat for 10–12 minutes until softened, stirring occasionally.

- Add the goats' cheese and continue to cook for 2 minutes, then season to taste.

- Roll out the pastry on a lightly floured surface to 1 cm (½ in) thickness and use it to line a fluted rectangular tart tin.

- Press into the base and sides and prick the base with a fork, then fill with the onion and cheese mixture.

- Bake for 30–35 minutes until the pastry is cooked through and golden at the edges, then remove to a wire rack to cool before serving.

TOP TIP
Use a pair of tongs to lift the onions and cheese onto the tart easily.

Salmon and Leek Turnovers

MAKES 4

PREPARATION TIME 20 MINUTES

COOKING TIME 40–45 MINUTES

INGREDIENTS

2 tbsp olive oil

½ large leek, halved, sliced and washed

salt and freshly ground black pepper

450 g / 1 lb / 3 cups skinless salmon fillet, diced

300 g / 10 ½ oz prepared puff pastry

a little plain (all-purpose) flour, for dusting

75 g / 3 oz / ½ cup smoked salmon slices

a small bunch of dill, torn

1 medium egg, beaten

1 lemon, cut into wedges

METHOD

- Heat the olive oil in a large frying pan set over a medium heat. Add the leek and a little salt, then sweat for 4–5 minutes until softened.

- Add the salmon and cook for 4–5 minutes, then season to taste and set to one side.

- Preheat the oven to 190°C (170°C fan) / 375F / gas 5 and line a baking tray with greaseproof paper.

- Roll out the pastry on a lightly floured surface to ½ cm (¼ in) thickness and cut out 4 rounds approximately 18 cm (7 in) in diameter.

- Spoon the leek and salmon onto the centre, followed by the smoked salmon and some dill.

- Wet the rim of the pastry with a little water, then fold the bottom end over the filling and seal against the opposite side.

- Arrange on the baking tray and score a pattern using a sharp knife, then brush with beaten egg.

- Bake for 20–25 minutes until the pastry is golden and cooked through. Serve with lemon wedges and more dill.

Crab Quiche

SERVES 6
PREPARATION TIME 15 MINUTES
COOKING TIME 30–35 MINUTES

INGREDIENTS

250 g / 9 oz prepared shortcrust pastry

a little plain (all-purpose) flour, for dusting

375 ml / 13 fl. oz / 1 ½ cups whole (full-fat) milk

250 ml / 9 fl. oz / 1 cup double (heavy) cream

4 large eggs

110 g / 4 oz / 1 cup Cheddar, grated

450 g / 1 lb / 3 cups cooked crabmeat

a small bunch of dill, finely chopped

salt and freshly ground black pepper

METHOD

- Preheat the oven to 180°C (160°C fan) / 350F / gas 4.

- Roll out the pastry on a lightly floured surface into a rectangle approximately 1 cm (½ in) thick and use it to line the base and sides of a fluted rectangular tart tin.

- Prick with a fork and chill as you prepare the filling.

- Whisk together the milk, cream, eggs and Cheddar in a mixing bowl, then add the crabmeat and dill and season to taste.

- Pour the filling into the lined pastry case. Bake for 30–35 until the pastry is cooked and the filling is just set.

- Remove to a wire rack to cool before turning out and serving.

TOP TIP

The quiche can be eaten cold. Cool to room temperature, then cover and chill.

Seafood Empanadas

MAKES 8

PREPARATION TIME 20 MINUTES

COOKING TIME 18–22 MINUTES

INGREDIENTS

400 g / 14 oz / 2 cups canned tuna chunks, drained and flaked

150 g / 5 oz / 1 cup cooked prawns (shrimp), chopped

150 g / 5 oz / 1 ½ cups feta

2 tbsp olive oil

1 lemon, juiced

salt and freshly ground black pepper

350 g / 12 oz prepared puff pastry

a little plain (all-purpose) flour, for dusting

1 large egg, beaten

½ tsp dried oregano

½ tsp dried tarragon

2 tbsp extra virgin olive oil

METHOD

- Preheat the oven to 190°C (170°C fan) / 350F / gas 5 and line a large baking tray with greaseproof paper.

- Mix together the tuna, prawns, feta, olive oil, lemon juice and seasoning in a large mixing bowl.

- Roll out the pastry on a lightly floured surface into a large round approximately ½ cm (¼ in) thick.

- Use a cookie cutter to stamp out rounds of pastry approximately 12 cm (5 in) in diameter.

- Spoon the seafood filling onto the centre of the rounds of pastry. Wet the rims with a little water and fold over to seal into empanadas.

- Lift onto a large baking tray and brush with the beaten egg. Sprinkle over the dried herbs, season and drizzle with extra virgin olive oil.

- Bake for 18–22 minutes until golden and puffed before serving.

TOP TIP

Twist the cookie cutter to help separate the rounds of dough away from the main pastry.

Sweet Pies

Apple Pie

SERVES 6

PREPARATION TIME 15 MINUTES

COOKING TIME 1 HOUR 5–10 MINUTES

INGREDIENTS

750 g / 1 lb 10 oz / 5 cups Bramley apples,
    peeled, cored and diced

1 tsp vanilla extract

a pinch of salt

175 g / 6 oz / ¾ cup caster (superfine) sugar

125 g / 4 ½ oz / ¾ cup plain (all-purpose)
    flour, plus extra for dusting

110 g / 4 oz / ½ cup unsalted butter, cold and
    cubed

350 g / 12 oz prepared shortcrust pastry

1 large egg, beaten

METHOD

- Preheat the oven to 180°C (160°C fan) / 350F / gas 4. Place the apples, vanilla extract and salt in a saucepan with half of the sugar and 2 tbsp of water.

- Cover and cook over a low heat, stirring occasionally until softened, then set to one side.

- Pulse the flour with the remaining sugar and butter in a food processor until the mixture resembles breadcrumbs.

- Roll out half the pastry on a lightly floured surface to approximately ½ cm (¼ in) thickness and use it to line the base and sides of a 20 cm (8 in) fluted pie dish.

- Prick the base with a fork, then sprinkle over half of the crumble mixture. Top with the apples and the rest of the crumble mixture.

- Roll out the remaining pastry to 1 cm (½ in) thickness, then drape over the top of the filling.

- Crimp the top against the lined pastry and cut away any excess, then brush the top with beaten egg and bore a small hole in the middle.

- Bake for 45–55 minutes until the pastry is golden and cooked, then serve.

Key Lime Pie

SERVES 6

PREPARATION TIME 15 MINUTES

CHILLING TIME 4 HOURS 20 MINUTES

INGREDIENTS

150 g / 5 oz / 1 cup digestive biscuits, crushed

100 g / 3 ½ oz / ½ cup butter, melted

4 large egg yolks

125 g / 2 ½ oz / 1 cup icing (confectioners')
    sugar

400 g / 14 oz / 2 cups condensed milk

3 limes, juiced and zested

whipped cream, to serve

METHOD

- Preheat the oven to 180°C (160°C fan) / 350F / gas 4.

- Combine the crushed biscuits and melted butter in a large mixing bowl until they resemble wet sand.

- Press the mixture into the base and sides of an 18 cm (7 in) springform tart tin. Bake for 10 minutes, then remove to a wire rack to cool.

- Beat the egg yolks and icing sugar in a large mixing bowl with an electric whisk, then add the condensed milk and beat thoroughly for 2–3 minutes until thick.

- Add the lime juice and most of the zest and beat again for 2–3 minutes before pouring into the base. Cover and chill the pie for 4 hours.

- Turn the pie out after chilling and serve slices with whipped cream and the remaining lime zest to garnish.

TOP TIP
When slicing the pie, warm a sharp knife under hot running water to cut evenly.

Spiced Plum Pie

SERVES 6

PREPARATION TIME 15 MINUTES

COOKING TIME 45–50 MINUTES

INGREDIENTS

300 g / 10 ½ oz prepared shortcrust pastry

a little plain (all-purpose) flour, for dusting

225 g / 8 oz / 1 cup Greek yoghurt, whipped

165 g / 5 ½ oz / 1 cup soft dark brown sugar

2 tsp ground cinnamon

1 tsp ground ginger

450 g / 1 lb / 3 cups plums, pitted and cut into wedges

METHOD

- Preheat the oven to 160°C (140°C fan) / 325F / gas 3.

- Roll out the pastry on a lightly floured surface into a round approximately 1 cm (½ in) thick.

- Use the pastry to line a 20 cm (8 in) fluted tart tin, pressing well into the base and sides.

- Prick with a fork and top with the whipped Greek yoghurt, then sprinkle over the sugar and ground spices.

- Top with the plum wedges and arrange them to fit, then bake for 45–50 minutes until the pastry is cooked through.

- Remove to a wire rack to cool, then turn out and serve.

TOP TIP

Mix together the spices in a small pot before sprinkling over the sugar.

Bakewell Pie

SERVES 6–8

PREPARATION TIME 20 MINUTES

COOKING TIME 40–45 MINUTES

INGREDIENTS

250 g / 9 oz prepared shortcrust pastry

55 g / 2 oz / ⅓ cup plain (all-purpose) flour, plus extra for dusting

225 g / 8 oz / 1 cup unsalted butter, softened

225 g / 8 oz / 1 cup caster (superfine) sugar

175 g / 6 oz / 1 ¾ cups ground almonds

3 large eggs

1 tsp vanilla extract

2 golden delicious apples, peeled, cored and thinly sliced

2 tbsp flaked (slivered) almonds

METHOD

- Preheat the oven to 180°C (160°C fan) / 350F / gas 4.

- Roll out the pastry on a lightly floured surface to ½ cm (¼ in) thickness and use it to line a 20 cm (8 in) tart tin, pressing well into the base and sides.

- Prick the pastry with a fork and set to one side, then beat together the flour, butter, sugar, ground almonds, eggs and vanilla extract in a large mixing bowl for 3–4 minutes with an electric whisk until thoroughly combined.

- Spoon the mixture into the pastry case and smooth with the back of a tablespoon.

- Top with a thin layer of apple slices and scatter over the flaked almonds.

- Bake for 40–45 minutes until the pastry and filling are cooked and golden.

- Remove to a wire rack to cool, then serve.

TOP TIP
The butter should be really soft before preparing the filling.

Individual Fruit Pies

MAKES 4

PREPARATION TIME 25 MINUTES

COOKING TIME 30–35 MINUTES

INGREDIENTS

350 g / 12 oz prepared shortcrust pastry

a little plain (all-purpose) flour, for dusting

450 g / 1 lb / 3 cups Bramley apples, peeled, cored and diced

150 g / 5 oz / 1 cup gooseberries

85 g / 3 ½ oz / ½ cup soft light brown sugar

2 large egg whites

110 g / 4 oz / ½ cup caster (superfine) sugar

½ tsp cream of tartar

150 g / 5 oz / 1 cup redcurrants

1 tbsp icing (confectioners') sugar, for dusting

METHOD

- Preheat the oven to 180°C (160°C fan) / 350F / gas 4. Roll out the pastry on a lightly floured surface to ½ cm (¼ in) thickness and cut out four rounds of pastry to line individual tartlet tins.

- Drape the pastry over the tins and press well into the base and sides, cutting away any excess.

- Line with greaseproof paper and fill with baking beans, then blind-bake for 12–15 minutes until golden at the edges.

- Remove to a wire rack to cool and discard the baking beans and greaseproof paper.

- Combine the apple, gooseberries, brown sugar and 2 tbsp of water in a saucepan, then cook over a low heat until the fruit is soft and mushy.

- Beat the egg whites in a large, clean mixing bowl until they form soft peaks. Add half the caster sugar and beat until thick and shiny.

- Add the cream of tartar and the remaining sugar and continue to beat until glossy, then spoon into a piping bag fitted with a star nozzle. Increase the oven to 220°C (220°C fan) / 425F / gas 7.

- Spoon the fruit compote into the pastry and pipe over swirls of meringue, then surround with redcurrants and bake for 15–18 minutes until the meringue is golden brown.

- Remove to a wire rack and leave to cool slightly, then dust with icing sugar to serve.

Banana and Chocolate Pie

SERVES 4

PREPARATION TIME 15 MINUTES

COOKING TIME 25 MINUTES

INGREDIENTS

200 g / 7 oz prepared shortcrust pastry

a little plain (all-purpose) flour, for dusting

1 small egg, beaten

250 g / 9 oz / 1 cup chocolate and hazelnut spread

2 large bananas, sliced

whipped cream, to serve

50 g / 2 oz / ⅓ cup dark chocolate

METHOD

- Preheat the oven to 190°C (170°C fan) / 375F / gas 5.

- Roll out the pastry on a lightly floured surface to ½ cm (¼ in) thickness and use it to line an 18 cm (7 in) straight-sided tart tin.

- Press the pastry into the base and sides before cutting away any excess.

- Prick the base with a fork and line with greaseproof paper, then fill with baking beans and blind bake for 12–15 minutes until golden brown.

- Remove from the oven and discard the beans and the greaseproof paper. Brush the base with the beaten egg and return to the oven for 4 minutes.

- Remove to a wire rack to cool slightly, then spread the chocolate and hazelnut spread over the base and top with slices of banana.

- Return to the oven for 2–3 minutes to glaze. Remove and leave to cool slightly, then turn out and serve with whipped cream and dark chocolate grated over.

TOP TIP
Warm the chocolate and hazelnut spread in a microwave to make it easier to spread.

Blueberry Pie

SERVES 6–8

PREPARATION TIME 10 MINUTES

COOKING TIME 30–35 MINUTES

INGREDIENTS

250 g / 9 oz prepared shortcrust pastry

a little plain (all-purpose) flour, for dusting

1 small egg, beaten

350 g / 12 oz / 1 ½ cups fromage blanc

350 g / 12 oz / 1 ½ cups vanilla yoghurt

1 tbsp lemon juice

½ tsp vanilla extract

runny honey, to drizzle

300 g / 10 ½ oz / 2 cups blueberries

METHOD

- Preheat the oven to 180°C (160°C fan) / 350F / gas 4. Roll out the pastry on a lightly floured surface into a round approximately ½ cm (¼ in) thick and use it to line the base and sides of a 20 cm (8 in) fluted tart tin.

- Trim any excess pastry and discard, then prick the base all over with a fork.

- Line the pastry with greaseproof paper and fill with baking beans before blind baking for 15–18 minutes until the edges are golden brown.

- Remove from the oven and discard the greaseproof paper and baking beans.

- Return the pastry to the oven for 4–5 minutes to brown the base.

- Remove again and brush with the beaten egg, then return to the oven for another 2 minutes. Remove to a wire rack to cool.

- Beat together the fromage blanc, yoghurt, lemon juice and vanilla extract in a large mixing bowl until smooth.

- Carefully remove the pastry from the tin and filling with the fromage blanc filling. Drizzle with some runny honey, then top with most of the blueberries and serve the remainder on the side.

Custard Cream Pie

SERVES 8

PREPARATION TIME 15 MINUTES

COOKING TIME 1 HOUR 20–25 MINUTES

INGREDIENTS

250 g / 9 oz prepared shortcrust pastry

a little plain (all-purpose) flour, for dusting

350 ml / 12 fl. oz / 1 ½ cups double (heavy) cream

250 ml / 9 fl. oz / 1 cup whole (full-fat) milk

2 tsp vanilla extract

4 large eggs

150 g / 5 oz / ⅔ cup caster (superfine) sugar

METHOD

- Preheat the oven to 180°C (160°C fan) / 350F / gas 4. Roll out the pastry on a lightly floured surface to 1 cm (½ in) thickness and use it to line a 20 cm (8 in) tart tin.

- Press well into the base and sides, cut away any excess pastry and prick the base with a fork.

- Line the pastry with greaseproof paper and fill with baking beans, then blind bake for 15 minutes. Remove to a wire rack and discard the greaseproof paper and beans.

- Return to the oven for 5 minutes before removing again and setting to one side.

- Reduce the oven temperature to 150°C (130°C fan) / 300F / gas 2 and combine the cream, milk and vanilla extract in a saucepan.

- Bring the cream mixture to the boil, then remove from the heat. Beat together the eggs and sugar in a heatproof bowl until thick and frothy.

- Whisk with the cream mixture until incorporated and smooth, then strain into a jug.

- Pour into the pastry case and bake for 50–60 minutes until set. Remove to a wire rack to cool before serving.

Cherry Pie

MAKES 4
PREPARATION TIME 30 MINUTES
COOKING TIME 40 MINUTES

INGREDIENTS

300 g / 10 ½ oz prepared shortcrust pastry

a little plain (all-purpose) flour, for dusting

400 g / 14 oz / 2 cups canned morello cherries, drained

2 tbsp whole (full-fat) milk

1 tbsp caster (superfine) sugar

METHOD

- Roll out two-thirds of the pastry on a lightly floured surface to approximately 1 cm (½ in) thickness and cut out four rounds to line the base and sides of the moulds of a cupcake tin.

- Line four moulds with the pastry and trim any excess pastry, then prick the bases and chill for 15 minutes.

- Preheat the oven to 180°C (160°C fan) / 350F / gas 4. Roll out the remaining pastry to the same thickness as before and cut out rounds of pastry approximately 5 cm (2 in) thick.

- Prick the pastry lids a few times with a fork, then remove the pastry from the fridge and fill with the cherries.

- Wet the rims of the lined pastry with a little water. Place the pastry lids on top and crimp the edges together to seal.

- Bake the pies for 30–35 minutes until the pastry is cooked and lightly golden, then whisk together the milk and sugar until the sugar has dissolved.

- Remove the pies from the oven and brush the tops with the glaze. Return to the oven for a few minutes to brown the glaze before serving.

SWEET PIES

Lemon Meringue Pie

SERVES 6–8
PREPARATION TIME 25 MINUTES
COOKING TIME 45 MINUTES

INGREDIENTS

250 g / 9 oz prepared shortcrust pastry

a little plain (all-purpose) flour, for dusting

450 g / 1 lb / 2 cups lemon curd

2 tbsp cornflour (cornstarch)

2 medium egg yolks

1 medium egg

3 medium egg whites, at room temperature

a pinch of salt

150 g / 5 oz / ⅔ cup caster (superfine) sugar

1 tsp cream of tartar

METHOD

- Preheat the oven to 190°C (170°C fan) / 375F / gas 5. Roll out the pastry on a floured surface to ½ cm (¼ in) thickness and use it to line an 18 cm (7 in) springform cake tin.

- Prick the pastry with a fork, then line with cling film and fill with baking beans. Blind bake for 15 minutes.

- Beat the lemon curd with 1 tbsp of water and half the cornflour in a saucepan, then cook over a low heat, stirring constantly, for 3–4 minutes.

- Beat in the egg yolks and whole egg until thickened, then remove from the heat and leave to cool.

- Whisk the egg whites and salt in a clean bowl until they form soft peaks. Add half the sugar and beat until stiff.

- Add the remaining sugar, cornflour and cream of tartar, continuing to beat until glossy.

- Fill the pastry with the curd mixture and spread the meringue on top in mounds.

- Bake for 20–25 minutes until golden on top, then remove from the oven and leave to cool before serving.

Fig Pie

SERVES 6

PREPARATION TIME 35 MINUTES

COOKING TIME 50–55 MINUTES

INGREDIENTS

225 g / 8 oz prepared shortcrust pastry

a little plain (all-purpose) flour, for dusting

2 large eggs

75 g / 3 oz / ⅓ cup caster (superfine) sugar

100 g / 3 ½ oz / ⅔ cup self-raising flour

150 ml / 5 fl. oz / ⅔ cup whole (full-fat) milk

½ tsp vanilla extract

2 tbsp unsalted butter, melted

450 g / 1 lb / 3 cups ripe figs, halved

a few sprigs of thyme, to garnish

METHOD

- Preheat the oven to 160°C (140°C fan) / 325F / gas 3.

- Roll out the pastry on a lightly floured surface to ½ cm (¼ in) thickness and use it to line a 20 cm (8 in) pie dish, pressing well into the base and sides.

- Trim any excess pastry and chill the pastry case for 20 minutes.

- Beat together the eggs and sugar in a mixing bowl until thick and frothy, then fold in the flour.

- Whisk in the milk, vanilla extract and melted butter in that order until you have a smooth batter.

- Pour the batter into the pastry case and arrange the fig halves on top.

- Bake for 50–55 minutes until the pastry is golden and the batter is set. Remove from the oven and garnish with thyme before serving.

TOP TIP

Ripe figs will feel soft to the touch, yielding with a little pressure when pressed.

Apple and Cherry Pie

SERVES 6–8

PREPARATION TIME 15–20 MINUTES

COOKING TIME 1 HOUR 15–20 MINUTES

INGREDIENTS

350 g / 12 oz prepared shortcrust pastry

a little plain (all-purpose) flour, for dusting

225 g / 8 oz / 2 cups ground almonds

110 g / 4 oz / ½ cup caster (superfine) sugar

150 g / 5 oz / ⅔ cup unsalted butter

2 small eggs

2 small egg whites

4 eating apples, peeled, cored and sliced

350 g / 12 oz / 2 ⅓ cups cherries, pitted

2 large egg yolks, beaten

METHOD

- Preheat the oven to 160°C (140°C fan) / 325F / gas 3. Roll out two-thirds of the pastry on a lightly floured surface to 1 cm (½ in) thickness.

- Line the base and sides of a 20 cm (8 in) pie dish with the pastry. Trim away the excess and prick the base with a fork, then chill.

- Pulse together the almonds, sugar, butter, eggs and egg whites in a food processor until smooth, then scrape into a mixing bowl.

- Add the apple slices and cherries and stir well to combine, then spoon into the lined pastry.

- Roll out the remaining pastry on a lightly floured surface to the same thickness as before, then drape over the filling and crimp against the lined pastry.

- Trim the excess pastry and brush the top with the beaten egg before scoring indents around the rim of the pastry.

- Bake for 1 hour until the pastry is golden and cooked through; the filling should be set.

- Remove to a wire rack to cool slightly before serving.

Raspberry Cream Pie

SERVES 4

PREPARATION TIME 15 MINUTES

COOKING TIME 20 MINUTES

INGREDIENTS

250 g / 9 oz prepared shortcrust pastry

a little plain (all-purpose) flour, for dusting

1 small egg, beaten

450 g / 1 lb / 2 cups mascarpone

65 g / 2 ½ oz / ½ cup icing (confectioners')
    sugar, plus extra for dusting

1 lemon, juiced

125 g / 4 ½ oz / 1 cup raspberries

METHOD

- Preheat the oven to 180°C (160°C fan) / 350F / gas 4.

- Roll out the pastry on a lightly floured surface to 1 cm (½ in) thickness and use it to line a 15 cm (6 in) fluted pie dish, pressing well into the base and sides.

- Cut away any excess pastry and prick the base with a fork.

- Line with greaseproof paper and fill with baking beans, then blind bake for 15 minutes.

- Remove from the oven and discard the beans and paper, then return to the oven for 2 minutes before removing again.

- Brush the base with the beaten egg and return to the oven for 2 minutes, then remove to a wire rack to cool.

- Beat together the mascarpone, icing sugar and lemon juice until smooth, then spoon into the cooled pastry case and top with raspberries.

- Dust with icing sugar before serving.

TOP TIP

Use a large balloon whisk to beat the mascarpone; this will give a lighter texture.

Pear Pie

SERVES 6–8

PREPARATION TIME 20 MINUTES

COOKING TIME 35–40 MINUTES

INGREDIENTS

350 g / 12 oz prepared puff pastry

a little plain (all-purpose) flour, for dusting

110 g / 4 oz / 1 cup ground almonds

110 g / 4 oz / ½ cup unsalted butter, softened

100 g / 3 ½ oz / ½ cup caster (superfine) sugar

1 small egg

1 small egg white

800 g / 1 lb 12 oz / 4 cups canned pear halves
    in juice, drained

2 large egg yolks

METHOD

- Preheat the oven to 180°C (160°C fan) / 350F / gas 4. Roll out two-thirds of the pastry on a lightly floured surface into a rectangle approximately ½ cm (¼ in) thick.

- Line the base and sides of a rectangular baking dish with the pastry. Prick the base with a fork and trim as necessary on the sides.

- Pulse together the almonds, butter, sugar, egg and egg white in a food processor until creamy, then spread out evenly across the base of the pastry.

- Top with the pear halves, then roll out the remaining pastry into a rectangle approximately ½ cm (¼ in) thick. Drape over the filling and seal against the sides of the pastry.

- Brush the top with the beaten egg yolk and bake for 35–40 minutes until golden brown all over.

- Remove from the oven and leave to stand briefly before serving.

TOP TIP

Reserve some of the pear juice from the cans and serve it with the pie.

Rhubarb Crumble

METHOD

- Preheat the oven to 180°C (160°C fan) / 350F / gas 4. Place the rhubarb, raspberries, vanilla extract and salt in a saucepan with half of the sugar and 2 tbsp of water.

- Cover and cook over a low heat, stirring occasionally until softened, then set to one side.

- Line a large rectangular baking dish with a sheet of greaseproof paper. Pulse the flour with the remaining sugar and butter in a food processor until the mixture resembles breadcrumbs.

- Roll out the pastry on a lightly floured surface to approximately 1 cm (½ in) thickness and use it to line the base and sides of the baking dish.

- Prick the base with a fork, then sprinkle over a quarter of the crumble mixture. Top with the fruit and the rest of the crumble mixture.

- Bake for 50–60 minutes until the pastry and crumble are golden and cooked, then serve immediately.

SERVES 6
PREPARATION TIME 10–15 MINUTES
COOKING TIME 1 HOUR 10–15 MINUTES

INGREDIENTS

600 g / 1 lb 5 oz / 4 cups rhubarb, trimmed and diced

175 g / 6 oz / 1 ½ cups raspberries

1 tsp vanilla extract

a pinch of salt

225 g / 8 oz / 1 cup caster (superfine) sugar

150 g / 5 oz / 1 cup plain (all-purpose) flour, plus extra for dusting

150 g / 5 oz / ⅔ cup unsalted butter, cold and cubed

300 g / 10 ½ oz prepared shortcrust pastry

TOP TIP
Discard any rhubarb leaves during preparation, as these can be toxic.

Summer Fruit Pie

METHOD

- Preheat the oven to 180°C (160°C fan) / 350F / gas 4. Roll out the pastry on a lightly floured surface to 1 cm (½ in) thickness and use it to line a 20 cm (8 in) fluted tart tin.

- Press the pastry well into the base and sides before removing any excess.

- Prick the pastry with a fork and line with greaseproof paper and baking beans. Blind bake for 15 minutes, then remove from the oven.

- Discard the beans and paper and return the pastry to the oven for 4–5 minutes until the base browns, then remove to a wire rack to cool.

- Meanwhile, soften the gelatine in the lemon juice and 1 tbsp of cold water for 5 minutes.

- Heat the mixture in a small saucepan over a low heat until the gelatine has dissolved.

- Beat together the cream cheese and the sugar in a large mixing bowl using an electric hand-held whisk for 2 minutes, then add the Greek yoghurt and the gelatine mixture and mix again until smooth.

- Add the vanilla extract and beat well before pouring into the pastry case.

- Cover and chill for 4 hours until set. Garnish the rim with the fruit and mint leaves before serving.

SERVES 6–8
PREPARATION TIME 25 MINUTES
COOKING TIME 25 MINUTES

INGREDIENTS

250 g / 9 oz prepared shortcrust pastry

a little plain (all-purpose) flour, for dusting

1 sheet of gelatine

1 lemon, juiced

400 g / 14 oz / 2 cups cream cheese

175 g / 6 oz / ¾ cup golden caster (superfine) sugar

275 g / 10 oz / 1 ¼ cups Greek yoghurt

2 tsp vanilla extract

150 g / 5 oz / 1 cup strawberries, hulled and halved

110 g / 4 oz / 1 cup blackberries

110 g / 4 oz / 1 cup raspberries

110 g / 4 oz / 1 cup blueberries

a small bunch of mint, leaves picked

Mince Pies

MAKES 4

PREPARATION TIME 20 MINUTES

COOKING TIME 25–30 MINUTES

INGREDIENTS

350 g / 12 oz prepared shortcrust pastry

a little plain (all-purpose) flour, for dusting

450 g / 1 lb / 2 cups mincemeat

1 tbsp caster (superfine) sugar

METHOD

- Preheat the oven to 180°C (160°C fan) / 350F / gas 4.

- Roll out the pastry on a lightly floured surface to ½ cm (¼ in) thickness and cut out 4 rounds to line fluted individual tartlet tins.

- Press the pastry into the base and sides, cutting away any excess pastry. Gather the excess and reroll to ½ cm (¼ in) thickness.

- Use a sharp knife to cut out 4 star shapes.

- Prick the bases of the lined pastry and fill with the mincemeat. Place a star of pastry on top and bake for 25–30 minutes until the pastry is cooked through.

- Remove to a wire rack and dust with caster sugar before serving.

TOP TIP

Warm the mincemeat before spooning into the pastry cases to make it easier to spread.

Sweet Tarts and Pastries

Chocolate Tart

METHOD

- Preheat the oven to 190°C (170°C fan) / 375F / gas 5. Roll out the pastry on a lightly floured surface to 1 cm (½ in) thickness and use to line a 20 cm (8 in) tart tin.

- Prick the base with a fork and line with greaseproof paper and baking beans.

- Blind-bake for 12–15 minutes until golden, then remove and discard the baking beans and paper.

- Brush with beaten egg and return to the oven for 5 minutes. Remove and leave to cool on a wire rack.

- Melt the chocolate, cream and liquid glucose in saucepan set over a medium heat, stirring until smooth.

- Remove from the heat, then beat in the butter and leave to cool for 5 minutes.

- Pour the chocolate filling into the pastry and chill for at least 2 hours before serving.

SERVES 6–8
PREPARATION TIME 20 MINUTES
COOKING TIME 25 MINUTES

INGREDIENTS

250 g / 9 oz prepared shortcrust pastry

a little plain (all-purpose) flour, for dusting

1 large egg, beaten

300 g / 10 ½ oz / 2 cups good-quality dark chocolate, chopped

250 ml / 9 fl. oz / 1 cup double (heavy) cream

1 tbsp liquid glucose

2 tbsp unsalted butter

TOP TIP
Sprinkle the tart with chopped mixed nuts before serving to add texture.

Apple Tart

SERVES 6

PREPARATION TIME 10–15 MINUTES

COOKING TIME 25–30 MINUTES

INGREDIENTS

200 g / 7 oz prepared shortcrust pastry

a little plain (all-purpose) flour, for dusting

4 golden delicious apples, peeled, cored and thinly sliced

1 lemon, juiced

110 g / 4 oz / ½ cup caster (superfine) sugar

2 tbsp unsalted butter, cold and cubed

METHOD

- Preheat the oven to 190°C (170°C fan) / 350F / gas 5.

- Roll out the pastry on a lightly floured surface to 1 cm (½ in) thickness. Invert a 20 cm (8 in) diameter plate onto the pastry and cut around it with a sharp knife.

- Line a baking tray with a sheet of greaseproof paper, then carefully lift the pastry round onto the paper.

- Prick with a fork, then toss the slices of apple with the lemon juice and sugar in a large mixing bowl.

- Overlap the slices on top of the pastry to cover it. Spoon over any juice and sugar in the bowl and dot with the butter.

- Bake for 25–30 minutes until the pastry is cooked through before serving.

TOP TIP

If slicing the apples ahead of time, dress with lemon juice to prevent browning.

Treacle Tart

SERVES 6–8

PREPARATION TIME 10–15 MINUTES

COOKING TIME 50–55 MINUTES

INGREDIENTS

250 g / 9 oz prepared shortcrust pastry

a little plain (all-purpose) flour

300 g / 10 ½ oz / 1 cup golden syrup, warmed

150 g / 5 oz / ½ cup treacle, warmed

225 g / 8 oz / 3 cups breadcrumbs

110 g / 4 oz / ½ cup clotted cream, to serve

METHOD

- Preheat the oven to 180°C (160°C fan) / 350F / gas 4.

- Roll out the pastry on a lightly floured surface to 1 cm (½ in) thickness and use it to line a 20 cm (8 in) springform tart tin.

- Press the pastry well into the base and sides before cutting away any excess.

- Prick the base with a fork, then line with greaseproof paper and baking beans. Blind bake for 15 minutes, then remove from the oven.

- Discard the beans and paper, then mix together the golden syrup, treacle and breadcrumbs in a mixing bowl and spoon into the pastry case.

- Bake for 35–40 minutes until set, then remove from the oven and leave to cool on a wire rack.

- Slice and serve with clotted cream on the side.

TOP TIP

Using stale bread for your breadcrumbs will produce the best results.

Cinnamon Pastry

MAKES 8

PREPARATION TIME 10 MINUTES

COOKING TIME 15–20 MINUTES

INGREDIENTS

250 g / 9 oz prepared puff pastry

a little plain (all-purpose) flour, for dusting

150 g / 5 oz / ⅔ cup caster (superfine) sugar

1 tbsp ground cinnamon

55 g / 2 oz / ¼ cup unsalted butter, melted

METHOD

- Preheat the oven to 190°C (170°C fan) / 375F / gas 5 and line a large baking tray with a sheet of greaseproof paper.

- Roll out the puff pastry on a lightly floured surface into a large rectangle approximately 1 cm (½ in) thick.

- Sprinkle over the sugar and cinnamon, spreading it out evenly over the pastry.

- Roll the rectangle into a sausage shape and brush with melted butter. Cut into 8 pieces and arrange, cut-side down, on the baking tray.

- Brush all over with more melted butter and bake for 15–20 minutes until puffed and golden.

- Remove to a wire rack to cool before serving.

TOP TIP

Chilled puff pastry is easier to work with than pastry that is room temperature.

Strawberry Freeform Tart

SERVES 6–8
PREPARATION TIME 20 MINUTES
COOKING TIME 20–25 MINUTES

INGREDIENTS

250 g / 9 oz prepared shortcrust pastry

a little plain (all-purpose) flour, for dusting

1 small egg, beaten

375 ml / 13 fl. oz / 1 ½ cups double (heavy) cream

1 tsp vanilla extract

100 g / 3 ½ oz / ¾ cup icing (confectioners') sugar, for dusting

300 g / 10 ½ oz / 2 cups strawberries, hulled and halved

METHOD

- Preheat the oven to 180°C (160°C fan) / 350F / gas 4. Roll out the pastry on a lightly floured surface into a round approximately 1 cm (½ in) thick and use it to line a 20 cm (8 in) fluted tart tin.

- Press well into the base and sides of the tin, trimming any excess pastry.

- Prick the base with a fork, then line with a sheet of greaseproof paper and fill with baking beans.

- Blind bake for 12–15 minutes until golden at the edges, then remove from the oven and discard the beans and paper.

- Return the pastry to the oven to brown for 3–4 minutes, then remove again and brush the base and sides with the beaten egg.

- Return to the oven for 2 minutes, then remove to a wire rack to cool as you prepare the filling.

- Whip the cream with the vanilla extract and most of the icing sugar in a mixing bowl until softly peaked.

- Remove the pastry from the tin and fill with the whipped cream. Top with strawberries and a dusting of icing sugar before serving.

Chocolate Eclairs

SERVES 12

PREPARATION TIME 25 MINUTES

COOKING TIME 45–50 MINUTES

INGREDIENTS

250 g / 9 oz prepared choux pastry

375 ml / 13 fl. oz / 1 ½ cups whole (full-fat) milk

1 vanilla pod, split lengthwise

4 medium egg yolks

55 g / 2 oz / ¼ cup caster (superfine) sugar

1 tbsp plain (all-purpose) flour

1 ½ tbsp cornflour (cornstarch)

250 ml / 9 fl. oz / 1 cup double (heavy) cream

300 g / 10 ½ oz / 2 cups dark chocolate, chopped

1 tbsp golden syrup

METHOD

- Preheat the oven to 160°C (140°C fan) / 325F / gas 3 and line a large baking tray with a sheet of greaseproof paper.

- Spoon the choux pastry into a piping bag fitted with a large, straight-sided nozzle. Pipe 15 cm (6 in) fingers of pastry onto the prepared baking tray, spaced apart.

- Bake for 30–35 minutes until golden brown and slightly puffed, then remove to a wire rack to cool.

- Combine the milk and vanilla pod in a saucepan. Bring to a simmer over a medium heat before removing to one side.

- Whisk together the egg yolks and sugar in a heatproof bowl until pale and thick, then sift in the flour and cornflour and whisk again briefly.

- Whisk over the warm milk in a slow, steady stream before pouring into a clean saucepan. Cook over a low heat for 2–3 minutes, stirring constantly, until thickened.

- Transfer the cream filling to a clean bowl, then cover and chill until cold.

- Once cold, spoon the filling into a piping bag fitted with a nozzle; bore a hole through the centre of the choux pastries and pipe the filling into them.

- Bring the cream to the boil in a saucepan. Pour over the chocolate and golden syrup in a bowl and leave for a minute before whisking until smooth.

- Leave to cool and thicken before spreading over the eclairs and serving.

203

Apricot and Almond Tart

SERVES 6–8

PREPARATION TIME 20 MINUTES

COOKING TIME 50–55 MINUTES

INGREDIENTS

275 g / 10 oz prepared shortcrust pastry

a little plain (all-purpose) flour, for dusting

225 g / 8 oz / 2 cups ground almonds

110 g / 4 oz / ½ cup caster (superfine) sugar

150 g / 5 oz / ⅔ cup unsalted butter

2 medium eggs

2 medium egg whites

350 g / 12 oz / 1 ¾ cups apricot jam (jelly)

3 tbsp flaked (slivered) almonds

METHOD

- Preheat the oven to 180°C (160°C fan) / 350F / gas 4. Roll out the pastry on a lightly floured surface to 1 cm (½ in) thickness and use it to line a 20 cm (8 in) tart tin.

- Press well into the base and sides before trimming any excess, overhanging pastry. Prick the base with a fork and chill.

- Prepare the filling by blitzing together the ground almonds, sugar and butter in a food processor until creamy. Add the eggs and egg whites and pulse well until combined.

- Fill the pastry case with the filling before topping with the apricot jam.

- Bake for 45–50 minutes until the pastry and filling are cooked. Top with the flaked almonds and return to the oven for 5 minutes.

- Remove to a wire rack to cool before turning out and serving.

TOP TIP
Warming the apricot jam before spreading it over the filling will make the task easier.

Egg Custard Tarts

MAKES 8

PREPARATION TIME 20 MINUTES

COOKING TIME 25 MINUTES

INGREDIENTS

300 g / 10 ½ oz prepared puff pastry

a little plain (all-purpose) flour, for dusting

350 ml / 12 fl. oz / 1 ½ cups whole (full-fat) milk

2 cm (1 in) stick of cinnamon

1 tsp vanilla extract

225 g / 8 oz / 1 cup caster (superfine) sugar

4 medium egg yolks, beaten

2 tbsp cornflour (cornstarch)

2 tbsp icing (confectioners') sugar

2 tsp ground cinnamon

METHOD

- Preheat the oven to 190°C (170°C fan) / 375F / gas 5. Roll out the pastry on a lightly floured surface to ½ cm (¼ in) thickness.

- Cut out 8 rounds and use them to line 8 individual fluted tartlet tins. Trim any excess overhanging pastry, then chill.

- Combine the milk, cinnamon stick and vanilla extract in a saucepan. Bring to a simmer over a moderate heat, then set to one side.

- Beat together the sugar and egg yolks in a heatproof bowl until pale and thick. Sift over the cornflour and beat again to incorporate.

- Pour a little of the hot milk over the egg yolk mixture, whisking well, then whisk in the remaining milk.

- Pour the mixture back into a clean saucepan and cook for 2–3 minutes over a low heat, stirring constantly, until thickened.

- Discard the cinnamon stick and let the custard cool a little before pouring into the pastry cases. Bake for 14–16 minutes until the pastry is golden and cooked.

- Remove to a wire rack to cool, then turn out and dust with icing sugar and ground cinnamon.

Orange Tart

SERVES 4

PREPARATION TIME 20 MINUTES

COOKING TIME 35–40 MINUTES

INGREDIENTS

150 g / 5 oz prepared shortcrust pastry

a little plain (all-purpose) flour, for dusting

2 large oranges

110 g / 4 oz / ½ cup unsalted butter, softened

100 g / 3 ½ oz / 1 cup ground almonds

100 g / 3 ½ oz / ½ cup caster (superfine) sugar

1 medium egg

½ tsp vanilla extract

METHOD

- Preheat the oven to 170°C (150°C fan) / 325F / gas 3. Roll out the pastry on a lightly floured surface to ½ cm (¼ in) thickness.

- Use it to line an 18 cm (7 in) straight-sided tart tin. Prick the base and trim any excess overhanging pastry.

- Slice one of the oranges and set to one side as a garnish; zest and juice the other into a mixing bowl.

- Add the softened butter, ground almonds, sugar, egg and vanilla extract and beat well until smooth and creamy.

- Spread the mixture evenly over the base of the pastry with a palette knife.

- Bake for 30–35 minutes until the pastry is cooked through and the filling is set, then preheat the grill to hot.

- Flash the tart under the hot grill to brown the top. Remove to a wire rack to cool before turning out.

- Slice and serve with the reserved orange slices.

TOP TIP
If you have a chef's blowtorch, you can use it to brown the top of the tart.

Tarte au Citron

SERVES 6–8

PREPARATION TIME 20 MINUTES

COOKING TIME 1 HOUR

INGREDIENTS

250 g / 9 oz prepared shortcrust pastry

a little plain (all-purpose) flour, for dusting

6 medium eggs

225 g / 8 oz / 1 cup golden caster (superfine) sugar

4 lemons, juiced and zested

125 ml / 4 ½ fl. oz / ½ cup double (heavy) cream

METHOD

- Preheat the oven to 180°C (160°C fan) / 350F / gas 4. Roll out the pastry on a lightly floured surface into a round approximately ½ cm (¼ in) thick.

- Use the pastry round to line a 20 cm (8 in) fluted tart tin. Press well into the base and sides, trimming any excess overhanging pastry.

- Prick the base with a fork and line with greaseproof paper before filling with baking beans. Blind-bake for 12–15 minutes until golden at the edges.

- Remove from the oven and discard the beans and paper, then return the pastry to the oven for 4–5 minutes.

- Remove again. Beat one of the eggs and use to brush the base and sides of the pastry, then return to the oven for 2 minutes.

- Remove to a wire rack to cool and reduce the oven to 160°C (140°C fan) / 324F / gas 3.

- Beat the remaining eggs with the sugar, lemon juice and zest in a large mixing bow until the sugar has dissolved.

- Stir in the cream, then strain into a jug and pour into the pastry case. Bake for 30–35 minutes until just set.

- Remove to a wire rack to cool before turning out and serving.

Pear and Chocolate Tart

SERVES 6
PREPARATION TIME 10–15 MINUTES
COOKING TIME 30–35 MINUTES

INGREDIENTS

225 g / 8 oz prepared puff pastry

a little plain (all-purpose) flour, for dusting

250 g / 9 oz / 1 cup chocolate and hazelnut spread

2 large conference pears, peeled, cored and sliced

1 digestive biscuit, crushed

METHOD

- Preheat the oven to 190°C (170°C fan) / 375F / gas 5. Line a 20 cm (8 in) round baking tray with a sheet of greaseproof paper.

- Roll out the pastry on a lightly floured surface into a 22 cm (9 in) round approximately 1 cm (½ in) thick.

- Lift onto the baking tray and prick the base with a fork.

- Spread the chocolate and hazelnut spread evenly over the pastry, leaving a 2 cm (1 in) border all the way around.

- Top with the pear slices and arrange them to fit as necessary, then fold the 2 cm (1 in) border back over the pear slices to make a rim.

- Bake for 20–25 minutes until the pastry is golden and cooked through.

- Remove to a wire rack to cool, then garnish with the crushed biscuit and serve.

TOP TIP

Use a warmed palette knife to spread the chocolate and hazelnut spread.

Raspberry Tarts

MAKES 8

PREPARATION TIME 20 MINUTES

COOKING TIME 20 MINUTES

INGREDIENTS

300 g / 10 ½ oz prepared shortcrust pastry

a little plain (all-purpose) flour, for dusting

300 g / 10 ½ oz / 2 ½ cups raspberries

50 g / 2 oz / ½ cup shelled pistachios, finely sliced

1 tbsp pumpkin seeds, crushed

1 tbsp icing (confectioners') sugar

METHOD

- Preheat the oven to 180°C (160°C fan) / 350F / gas 4.

- Roll out the pastry on a lightly floured surface to ½ cm (¼ in) thickness. Cut out 8 ovals of pastry and use them to line 8 individual oval fluted tartlet tins.

- Prick the bases with a fork and line with greaseproof paper, then fill with baking beans and blind bake for 12–14 minutes until golden brown.

- Remove from the oven and discard the beans and paper, then return to the oven for 3–4 minutes to brown the bases.

- Remove to a wire rack to cool.

- Once cool, fill with the raspberries, arranging them to fit neatly in each tart.

- Top with the sliced pistachios and crushed pumpkin seeds. Dust lightly with icing sugar before serving.

TOP TIP

A tea strainer is good for dusting individual pastries and tarts with icing sugar.

Chocolate and Hazelnut Tart

SERVES 6

PREPARATION TIME 20 MINUTES

COOKING TIME 25 MINUTES

INGREDIENTS

225 g / 8 oz prepared shortcrust pastry

a little plain (all-purpose) flour, for dusting

350 ml / 12 fl. oz / 1 ½ cups double (heavy) cream

1 tbsp liquid glucose

300 g / 10 ½ oz / 2 cups dark chocolate, chopped

225 g / 8 oz / 2 cups hazelnuts (cobnuts)

METHOD

- Preheat the oven to 180°C (160°C fan) / 350F / gas 4. Roll out the pastry on a lightly floured surface into a round approximately ½ cm (¼ in) thick.

- Use the round of pastry to line an 18 cm (7 in) tart tin. Press well into the base and sides before trimming any excess, overhanging pastry.

- Prick the base with a fork and line with greaseproof paper, then fill with baking beans and blind-bake for 12–15 minutes until golden at the edges.

- Remove from the oven and discard the beans and paper, then return to the oven for 4–5 minutes to brown the base.

- Remove to a wire rack to cool.

- Combine the cream and liquid glucose in a saucepan. Bring to the boil before removing to one side.

- Pour over the chocolate in a heatproof bowl and leave for 1 minute, then whisk until smooth.

- Leave to cool and thicken slightly.

- Arrange the hazelnuts in the base of the pastry before topping with the chocolate filling. Leave to set before serving.

Apple Strudel

SERVES 6–8

PREPARATION TIME 15 MINUTES

COOKING TIME 30–40 MINUTES

INGREDIENTS

350 g / 12 oz prepared puff pastry

a little plain (all-purpose) flour, for dusting

750 g / 1 lb 10 oz / 5 cups eating apples,
    peeled, cored and diced

100 g / 3 ½ oz / ⅔ cup raisins

110 g / 4 oz / ½ cup caster (superfine) sugar

2 tsp ground cinnamon

½ tsp ground nutmeg

1 lemon, juiced

1 large egg, beaten

3 tbsp flaked (slivered) almonds

2 tbsp icing (confectioners') sugar, for dusting

METHOD

- Preheat the oven to 190°C (170°C fan) / 375F / gas 5 and grease and line a large baking tray with greaseproof paper.

- Roll out the pastry on a lightly floured surface into a 30 x 20 cm (12 x 8 in) rectangle approximately ½ cm (¼ in) thick.

- Toss together the apples, raisins, sugar, ground spices and lemon juice in a large mixing bowl.

- Spoon the filing evenly down one side of the pastry so that it is offset from the centre. Leave a 2 cm (1 in) border on the side of the pastry with the filling.

- Brush the whole border with beaten egg and fold the pastry over the filling to meet the other border, sealing well.

- Carefully lift onto the baking tray and brush the top with beaten egg. Sprinkle over the flaked almonds.

- Bake for 30–40 minutes until the pastry is golden and cooked through. Remove to a wire rack to cool.

- Dust with icing sugar before slicing and serving.

219

INDEX

VINEGAR, BALSAMIC
Cheese and Tomato Tarts, 131

WINE, RED
Beef and Onion Pie, 23
Lamb, Pea and Potato Pie, 47

WINE, WHITE
Individual Fish Pie, 91
Salmon and Prawn Pie, 80
Smoked Salmon and Herb Pie, 76
Smoked Trout Fish Pie, 88

YOGHURT
Blueberry Pie, 168
Potato and Curry Samosas, 139
Spiced Plum Pie, 160
Summer Fruit Pie, 187